151

Quick Ideas

to

Deal With
Difficult People

151

Quick Ideas

to

Deal With
Difficult People

By Carrie Mason-Draffen

CAREER
PRESS

Franklin Lakes, NJ

151 Quick Ideas to Deal With Difficult People
Edited by and Typeset by Kate Henches
Cover design by Ark Stein/Visual Group
Printed in the U.S.A. by Book-mart Press

To order this title, please call toll-free 1-800-CAREER-1 (NJ and Canada: 201-848-0310) to order using VISA or MasterCard, or for further information on books from Career Press.

CAREER
PRESS

The Career Press, Inc., 3 Tice Road, PO Box 687,
Franklin Lakes, NJ 07417
www.careerpress.com

Library of Congress Cataloging-in-Publication Data
Mason-Draffen, Carrie, 1951-
    151 quick ideas to deal with difficult people / by Carrie Mason-Draffen.
        p. cm.
    Includes index.
    ISBN-13: 978-1-56414-938-1
    ISBN-10: 1-56414-938-2
    1. Problem employees. 2. Conflict management. 3. Personnel management. I. Title. II. Title: One hundred fifty one quick ideas to deal with difficult people. III. Title: One hundred and fifty one quick ideas to deal with difficult people.

HF5549.5.E42M384 2007

650.1′3—dc22   2006100140

Contents

How to Use This Book

Every quick idea in this book has been selected to directly or indirectly help you confront conflicts and mediate disputes, encourage communication and stop toxic talk, and identify and solve problems before they occur.

Don't try to implement all 151 ideas at once, because some won't be a good fit right now. Read through all 151 quick ideas and select only those that can really make a difference. Label your ideas:

- ◆ Implement now.
- ◆ Review again in 30 days.
- ◆ Pass the idea along to_____.

Involve your staff in selecting and implementing these ideas, and don't forget to give credit for their success! Invest in additional copies of this book and distribute them among your staff. Get everyone involved in selecting and recommending various quick ideas.

Revisit this book every 90 days. As your business changes, you will find new quick ideas that might suit you better now that competition is heating up.

Remember: All the ideas in this book have been proven in businesses across the United States and around the world. They have worked for others and will work for you!

Establish a Zero-Tolerance Policy

When it comes to problem employees, your most powerful tool is a zero-tolerance policy. Establishing such a policy—and adhering to it—ensures that you will address inappropriate behavior consistently and decisively.

Adhering to the policy is crucial. A major New York corporation noted its zero-tolerance policy in defending itself against a sexual-harassment lawsuit filed by a female employee. But the company didn't follow its own rules and a federal agency found in favor of the woman.

Your zero-tolerance policy should make it clear that the rules apply to everyone, from executives to

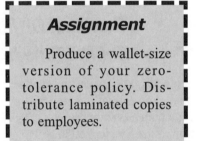

Assignment

Produce a wallet-size version of your zero-tolerance policy. Distribute laminated copies to employees.

janitors. Such a policy calls for you to give all accusations of inappropriate behavior a full airing, even if they are swirling around your star salesperson.

You should make sure everyone in the company knows your policy. Distribute copies and require employees to sign and return an enclosed sheet acknowledging receipt.

Peter Handal, president and chief executive officer of Dale Carnegie Training in Hauppauge, New York, said that because of their importance, zero-tolerance policies should be communicated in more than one media: in a manual, via e-mail, and in meetings. He recommends that you revisit the policy at least every six months.

"If you just talk about things like that once a year, they're not as important to people," says Carnegie. "It gets repetitive, but that is the way to learn the message."

Epilogue

A zero-tolerance policy is like a moral compass. If you ignore the direction to which it's pointing, you'll lose your way.

2

Don't Let Difficult People Set the Tone for the Office

Kathy supervises the support staff at a medium-sized company. She sought my advice because she was at the end of her rope with a defiant secretary. The employee set her own hours. She routinely clocked in at 9:30 a.m., a half hour later than the office starting time. And she clocked out at 5:30 p.m., a half hour past quitting time.

To make matters worse, the woman often spent the last hour of her shift socializing. Kathy repeatedly directed her to clock out when she finished her work. But the employee ignored the requests and continued to schmooze until her "personal" quitting time. One day Kathy threatened to clock her out. But the employee shot back with, "That's illegal." And she was right.

Assignment

If you have trouble rooting out unproductive work habits in your office, resolve today to seek an expert's help.

The situation deteriorated even more when other staff members began to follow the woman's lead. Kathy wanted to fire her. But the company owner nixed that because her work was "up to par." Kathy was losing the emotional tug of war.

Still, she wanted to reclaim control. So she reached out for help. I advised Kathy that since the secretary, who is paid hourly, is clearly lollygagging past the official quitting time, the company doesn't have to pay her for that time. After all, the company isn't forcing her to extend her hours. Her talk became cheap, even free for Kathy.

Kathy must keep detailed records to explain the discrepancy between the time clock and the woman's pay, just in case the uncooperative secretary files a complaint with the Labor Department. But after all those skirmishes, Kathy might even find extra paperwork welcome relief indeed.

Epilogue

When problem employees re-interpret your office practices, it's not your office anymore. It's theirs.

3

Bone Up on Dealing With Difficult Employees

You don't have to run off to get a degree in psychology to learn how to deal with problem employees. But you should avail yourself of some knowledge.

In the past few years, several high-profile company executives who were tried on corruption charges claimed they were out of the loop when their subordinates committed malfeasance. Those I-had-no-clue executives proved in spectacular fashion how much an uninformed manager has on the line when it comes to problem employees.

Assignment

Read through this book and apply its information to your workplace. Supplement the advice here with books from business best seller lists in newspapers or online.

They can ruin your business, drive away customers, and disrupt the office dynamic. If you feel at a total loss about tackling such problems, try a little knowledge. Take a seminar on resolving personnel conflicts, read a book, collect information online, or listen to a tape or CD.

Even if you decide to seek legal advice, you'll benefit more from the encounter if you bring something to the table. Effective managers bone up on unfamiliar topics just to make sure they ask the right questions.

If a lack of time is preventing you from being proactive in personnel matters, start with Steve Leveen's *The Little Guide to Your Well-Read Life*, a slender book that offers strategies on how to find interesting books, how to size them up quickly, and how to retain what you read. Reading to learn is a great way to invest in your employees, your company, and yourself.

Epilogue

"Ignorance is bliss," the saying goes, but not when it comes to personnel problems.

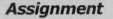

Don't Wait for the Boston Tea Party

If an employee asks your help in dealing with a difficult colleague, investigate the matter promptly and follow up with a solution. Worse than a problem employee is a manager who won't address intraoffice conflicts. He won't confront bullies or saboteurs. He believes both problems and people will self-correct.

When you take that approach you aggravate the problem and, worse, you lose credibility with your subordinates. If a team is involved, members may take matters into their own hands like the colonists who staged the Boston Tea Party more than 200 years ago because King George refused to correct the problem of taxation without representation. With your reputation as a do-nothing boss, insurrectionists in the office will refuse to cooperate. And they will refuse to continue to do the extra work that might have won you a promotion to management in the first place. At worst, the exasperated employees will go to your boss for relief. If that happens, as with King George, who had to surrender the colonies, your power will be diminished forever.

> ### *Assignment*
>
> If an employee asks you to intervene in a dispute, don't keep the person hanging. Set a date for a follow-up meeting as soon as possible.

No company needs a manager who won't manage. That approach damages morale and productivity. So when the complaints roll in, get yourself a cup of tea and go to work on a plan of attack.

> **Epilogue**
>
> *To paraphrase that time-honored quotation, "Time and tide wait for no managers."*

5

Be a Good Listener

One Father's Day, the minister of my church gave a sermon praising her father for helping to lift her out of a dreary situation. A seminary had offered her a full scholarship. But she visited the campus and found it lifeless. On the other hand, her first choice for school was a prestigious school with a bustling campus where students engaged in spirited debates. To go there, she would have to pay for her education with student loans. Because she didn't want to face a pile of debt after graduation, she felt she had no choice but to accept the offer from the less appealing school.

When she told her father about her Hobson's choice, he presented another scenario. If she attended the prestigious

> **Assignment**
>
> As an employee talks to you about a personnel conflict, take notes to keep your mind focused on the discussion rather than your next meeting.

school, she would mostly likely find a well-paying job after graduation. That would enable her to repay the loans. That insight buoyed her. She took out the loans, attended the school, and did, indeed, find a great job.

Her dad exemplified a good listener. He didn't judge her. Instead, he just heard her out and then graciously suggested an option she hadn't considered.

Good managers serve the same function. They don't judge when an employee seeks advice on how to resolve a conflict. Instead, they help subordinates see the problem in a different light.

That open-minded approach will serve you particularly well in tense, one-on-one meetings with employees. When you listen, they will know you take them seriously. It's hard for them to argue with that.

Epilogue

"Hearing is one of the body's five senses. But listening is an art."—Frank Tyger

---

6

Work Out a Solution Jointly

As a parent of teenagers, I know that negotiation always precedes persuasion. If I allow them to help shape the rules, they are more likely to buy into them. A top-down approach doesn't work with an age group so naturally prone to rebellion.

> **Assignment**
>
> If a corrective plan of action is top heavy with your ideas, make room for more input from employees. It should be their "Declaration of Interdependence," not yours.

Teenagers aren't the only group from whom the stakeholder approach works. Employees will embrace a policy if they have a say in it. If you take the top-down approach with office troublemakers, you will perpetuate a problem or exacerbate it.

Seek the employees' input from the very beginning before you draw up a corrective plan of action. You may seethe at such a suggestion. It may strike you as capitulation. But playing dictator won't get you the behavioral changes you're looking for, either.

In *Quiet Leadership: Six Steps to Transforming Performance at Work,* David Rock says, "Letting people come to their own insights when things haven't gone well is more comfortable for everyone and is more likely to deliver the outcome everyone wants: learning and behavior change for the next time."

So ask slackers about their new strategies for getting to work on time and what you can do to help. You'll empower them to think and work in a way that's more helpful to all.

Epilogue

To win employees' hearts and minds, give them a say.

7

Follow Through on a Plan of Action

"Visions that stay in the stars are visions that were poorly executed," says John Baldoni in *How Great Leaders Get Great Results*. An unexecuted or poorly executed plan to change an employee's behavior really is no better than wishful thinking.

Once you and an employee have drawn up a blueprint for corrective action, monitor its execution strategically. The best way is with follow-up meetings. Face to face is the best approach. An employee might dress up his or her progress in a written report. Meet regularly with the employee to gauge his or her progress.

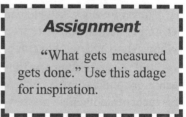

Assignment

"What gets measured gets done." Use this adage for inspiration.

Try meeting weekly after a crisis and then schedule the meetings less frequently as the employee makes progress. Keep the meetings short and on point. Ask for updates on new strategies. Consider scheduling the meetings during a coffee break or lunchtime on occasion to make doubly sure they take place. When you're running a business, time is one of your most precious resources and it often has to do double duty if you want to get things done.

The follow-up meetings convey the message that a plan of action is important to you and that you expect results. And you wouldn't want it any other way.

> **Epilogue**
>
> *Unless you execute it, your plan is no better than scrap paper.*

8

What Personality Trait Is at Play?

When my son was in elementary school, I tried coercion to get him to remember to turn in his homework. I resorted to yelling at him and revoking his privileges.

I did so out of utter frustration. I corrected the homework each night and assumed he turned it in the next day. So when his teacher told me his grades were slipping because he hadn't turned in his homework, I was livid.

> **Assignment**
>
> Follow Dale Carnegie's advice and try to understand the motivations behind employees' problem behaviors.

I demanded that he tell my why. He said he couldn't find it when the teacher asked for it. I thought the excuse was lame and banned video games and television.

The problem persisted until I read an article with excerpts from Dr. Mel Levine's book, *A Mind at a Time,* which focuses on the different ways that children learn based on how they perceive reality. My son suffered from "material management dysfunction," I learned. When confronted with the jumbled contents of his book bag, he felt helpless to wrest anything from it. I conferred with the school psychologist and we both agreed that after help-ing him with homework, I should help him organize his book bag for the next day. The homework problem ended.

The moral of the story holds truths for office situations as well. Once you understand a difficult employee's behavior, you can help find lasting solutions. Dale Carnegie says it best in *How to Win Friends and Influence People*: "There is a reason why the other man thinks and acts as he does. Ferret out that reason—and you have the key to his actions, perhaps his personality."

Epilogue

"You do not lead by hitting people over the head—that's assault not leadership."—Dwight Eisenhower

---

9

Make Sure the Employee Understands

At times my cowork-ers' version of a staff meeting differs so dramati-cally from mine that I won-der if we attended the same meeting. In essence, our own assumptions and interpretations produced the conflicting messages. That's why follow-up

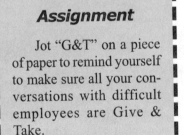

Assignment

Jot "G&T" on a piece of paper to remind yourself to make sure all your con-versations with difficult employees are Give & Take.

questions are so important. They allow a manager to clear up ambiguities.

When you're dealing with a problem employee, ambiguity is something you want to avoid at all cost. Does the person understand that getting to work on time means being at his or her desk at 9 a.m. and not pulling into the parking lot? Does the person understand that the job consists of more than what he or she wants to focus on?

Clear communication is a give and take. Encourage the employee to ask questions during a one-on-one meeting to address your concerns about his or her performance. And you should ask questions of the employee. Gauge whether the person understood you by asking his or her opinion of what you said. At the end of the meeting summarize the major points, and follow up the conversation with a memo documenting those points.

Save time, effort, and frustration by making sure an employee understands what you expect.

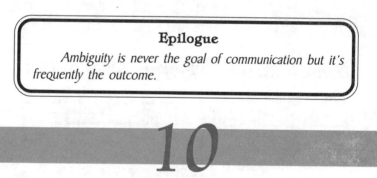

Epilogue

Ambiguity is never the goal of communication but it's frequently the outcome.

10

Try Humor

Too bad doctors don't prescribe a daily dose of laughter for working people—more of us might have that nice day everyone wishes for us.

"Studies prove that most encounters will run more smoothly, last longer, have more positive outcomes, and dramatically improve relationships when you make a point of regularly smiling and laughing to the point where it becomes a habit," authors Allan and Barbara Pease write in *The Definitive Book of Body Language*.

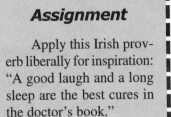

Assignment

Apply this Irish proverb liberally for inspiration: "A good laugh and a long sleep are the best cures in the doctor's book."

Apply judicious amounts of humor to your conversations. If you're having a tense conversation with an employee, humor will break the tension. Humor is also a great conversation starter when you're at a loss about how to begin a difficult discussion.

It carries a serious warning, though. You should never use it at the employee's expense. And don't overuse it. If you do, the employee may wonder if you were working on a stand-up comedy routine.

When served up in healthy portions, though, humor could be just what the doctor should have ordered.

Epilogue

Even the most serious talks benefit from a little humor.

11

Express Confidence That the Person Can Change

It's axiomatic that if you believe your employees can change, they are more likely to do so. If you believe they can change, make sure you let them know it. Like an energy drink, your encouraging words will boost their spirits.

Change is difficult. When a subordinate tries to move from negative territory into positive, he battles deeply ingrained habits. That fight will provoke anxiety. Counter that with a vote of confidence when the employee displays responsible behavior; speak up or drop the employee a note.

Management consultant John Maxwell advises leaders to play the "positive prophet" for their employees to ensure success.

"People need to hear you tell them that you believe in them and want them to succeed," Maxwell says in *Leadership 101: What every leader needs to know*.

Expand that network of praise by passing along positive feedback you receive from the employee's co-workers who have noticed or benefited from his changing ways. The payoff for you is the satisfaction that comes from having a hand in turning so many negatives into positives.

Assignment

Send a note or e-mail of thanks today to an employee who has shown improved behavior.

Epilogue

"No matter how old a mother is, she watches her middle-aged children for signs of improvement."—Writer Florida Scott-Maxwell

---

12

Thank Them for Their Cooperation

My family always thanks me when they really like a meal I prepare. Though preparing meals is my job (I am the chef of the family), their gratitude inspires me to keep looking for the "wow" factor in cooking.

That same dynamic works in the office. Even though employees are paid to work, they want to be thanked. As philosopher William James said, "The deepest principle in human nature is the craving to be appreciated."

Yet, too many companies underestimate the power of "Thank You." In a recent Gallup poll, fewer than 1/3 of American workers strongly agreed that they've received any praise from a supervisor in the last seven days. That adds up to a lot of missed opportunities to acknowledge good work.

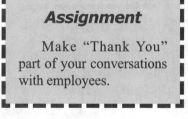

Assignment

Make "Thank You" part of your conversations with employees.

The beauty of gratitude is that it inspires employees to do more than just get by. And it will inspire employees who are improving to keep striving. All those efforts strengthen the bottom line. So if an employee with a record of chronic absenteeism puts together six months of perfect attendance, thank her. That's not capitulation, as some bosses may see it; that's a strategic move to encourage good habits.

Epilogue

Gratitude is an investment. If you give it, you will reap the dividends.

13

Master the Art of Difficult Conversations

The moment has arrived. You have to tell an employee that her work is unacceptable. You feel discomfort building. You anticipate a torrent of recriminations. As in the past, she will say everyone is picking on her. It could get ugly. It won't if you remain calm.

"Steady as she goes," was the *Star Trek* captain's command to the helmsman as he steered the Starship Enterprise through cosmic battles. An accuser will throw everything at you. But the person will run out of steam more quickly if you exhibit a steady hand.

> **Assignment**
>
> When you feel tense in a difficult situation, take a cue from yoga and focus on your breathing.

Vernice Givens, the president and owner of V&G Marketing Associates in Kansas City, Missouri, fired an employee who

16

Seek Other Owners' Advice

You don't need to reinvent the wheel when it comes to [dea]ling with difficult employees. Many others have gone [dow]n this road. Some surveys estimate that managers spend as much as 30 percent of their time managing conflict. Why not benefit from their experience?

Learning to deal with problem employees is really no different from any other aspect of your business. Whether you're trying to improve your marketing or cus[t]omer service, you'll always want to choose the most efficient means to your goal. A fellow owner could get you to the [f]inish line faster, yet small-business owners seem reluctant to [s]eek out information on personnel matters. In a survey en[t]itled Advice and Advisors, the National Federation of Inde[p]endent Business found that human resources and personnel were the two topics small business owners were least likely to seek advice about. Maybe that's why I get so many letters from their employees.

Try a different approach. Seek other business owners' advice while at trade association meetings. Seek out would-be mentors in personnel matters at your local chamber of

> **Assignment**
>
> Attend your community's next chamber of commerce meeting. During a question-and-answer period, ask advice on a personnel problem.

---

wasn't a team player. The woman reacted with threats of violence. Vernice remained calm. "The calmness made all the difference," she said. "It left her pretty much arguing with herself."

If the employee becomes insubordinate, end the conversation and tell her you will resume it at a later date when things calm down. Your objective is a win-win situation until an employee seems unredeemable for your company. Until that point, it's "Steady as she goes."

> **Epilogue**
> When hit with heavy weather on the job, take shelter by remaining calm.

14

Train Your Managers in the Art of Difficult Conversations

Even if you're a hands-on owner, your managers will have to confront difficult employees at some point. Make sure the supervisors have the training to steer through stressful conversations. Those talks are too important to be left to chance.

> **Assignment**
>
> Check with your managers on occasion to ask how they handled a difficult situation with a subordinate.

A manager trained in conflict resolution won't blow up and say something an employee can construe as discrimination or sexual harassment.

"A lot of it is your choice of words, your tone of voice, and making sure you address the performance as opposed to making the employee himself feel threatened," said Diane Pfadenhauer, the owner of Employment Practices Advisors in Northport, New York.

If your company has a human-resource department, ask the specialists there to conduct the training. Or, if you regularly confer with an employment lawyer, ask him or her to put together a one-day seminar on how to handle difficult employees.

It takes just one blunder to pull a company into a legal quagmire. Yet it takes such a small investment to prevent that from happening.

Epilogue

Give your managers the communications tools they need.

15

Don't Promote Mediocrity

Like Doctor Frankenstein, some employers create their own problem employees.

They promote people to jobs for credentials and experience. And they when resentment builds among empl work harder to make up for the new bos

The Frankenstein employee rises on the strength of his or her soft skills. of gab and they are superb networkers.

In an online poll, *HR.BLR.com* asked managers why they were forced to hir wouldn't have otherwise considered. Thi cited cronyism, by far the most prevalent reason.

Mediocrity begets mediocrity. If a manager can get ahead by doing minimal work, other employees may wonder why they should exert themselves. And certainly, the manager, with zero credibility, won't be able to persuade them to do

Assign

Make of skills you're lo a candidate. swayed from charming interv

Doctor Frankenstein created a life, but a for others. An office Frankenstein isn't much

---

Epilogue

Always look for the best talent or your choice back to haunt you.

---

commerce or alumni association meetings. Managing personnel conflicts can be a treacherous road to travel. You have no reason to go it alone.

Epilogue

If the personnel advice is free, you've got nothing to lose by seeking it out.

17

Reign in Difficult Family Members

Sarah worked as a business coordinator for a private school. She chose the school because it was family owned and thought the atmosphere would be collegial. But just weeks into her new job, the owner sent her inappropriate e-mails and propositioned her. She went to the head of HR. But the woman, who is the owner's cousin, simply said, "That is just the way he is."

Sarah quit and filed a sexual harassment complaint. If the head of HR had stood up to her cousin, the legal action might have been prevented.

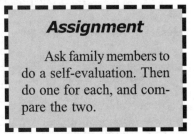

Assignment

Ask family members to do a self-evaluation. Then do one for each, and compare the two.

You should hold family members in your business to the same standards as everyone else. According to the *Wall Street Journal*, media mogul Ted Turner had no problem letting his son go, and firing him over dinner with, "You're toast."

You may have to take that step if family members believe they are entitled to come to work when they want to or just aren't up to the job.

"The first rule is that family members do not work in the business unless they are at least as able as any non-family employee, and work at least as hard," said management guru Peter Drucker in *The Daily Drucker: 366 days of insight and motivation for getting the right things done.*

It's especially important to monitor the behavior of family members at work. If they are abusive, employees may be reluctant to speak up. Make it clear to everyone that when it comes to work, blood isn't always thicker than water.

Epilogue
On the job, your family members are, first and foremost, your employees.

18

Mean What You Say

Jessie, a very active little girl, proved to be more than her mother could handle while they waited in line at a deli during the busy lunch hour. The mother held a baby in her arms and tried to keep track of Jessie, who was determined to explore.

"Jessie, I'll give you a cookie if you stand in line," the mother said.

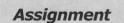

Assignment

If a problem employee asks permission to work at home occasionally, require that his performance improve and keep records to gauge his success.

"Okay," Jessie agreed. Seconds later, she was roaming the deli.

She was so busy flitting about and grabbing chips and other things nearby at one point that she mistakenly grabbed my leg as I stood in line ahead of the family.

Each time the girl escaped from the line, the mother reiterated her cookie rewards plan. Finally they made their way to the cash register and the desserts. As a cashier was bagging my order, I overhead the mother ask, " Jessie, what kind of cookie would you like?"

Jessie got her cookies. She also learned a bad lesson: Mommy doesn't always mean what she says.

That kind of credibility gap can be disastrous when dealing with problem employees. If they don't believe they should take your demands for better performances seriously, then you'll hold no more sway over them than Jessie's mom did over her.

Epilogue

Mind the credibility gap when dealing with problem employees.

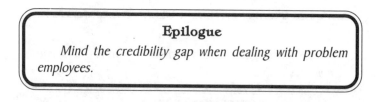

19
Handling Resistance to Overtime

Because of economic uncertainty, employers are reluctant to hire. As a result, they demand more of their existing staff. That means longer workdays. A worker called me to ask if it was legal for his boss to extend employees' quitting time by an hour and require them to take a two-hour lunch so the

Assignment

When the overtime piles up, remind employees of the flexible options you're willing to offer.

company avoids paying overtime. It's legal. But such demands come at a time when numerous surveys show that employees with families crave a work/life balance more than ever.

So you can expect resistance. Sure you could fire resisters. But that's not leadership; that's churning. Show leadership by offering employees some flexibility. If you ask them to work late one day, give them the option of coming in at a later time the next day. If necessary allow them leave for a few hours in the middle of the day to take care of things they normally would have tended to on the way home. And provide dinner from time to time when the office has to work late. Most of all , assure your staff you will do everything you can to minimize the overtime. Your employees will appreciate your concern and generosity.

Epilogue

Make overtime a win-win situation for you and your employees

20

Dealing With Information Hoarders

One of the many lessons learned from 9/11 was the importance of sharing information. Congress faulted the FBI and CIA for not pooling the results of their separate investigations. While that is an extreme example of what happens when the free flow of information is interrupted, it's, nonetheless, a potent reminder of the importance of making sure that key information reaches its destination.

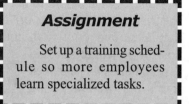

Assignment

Set up a training schedule so more employees learn specialized tasks.

Some experts refer to information as "workplace currency." And just like currency, information is meant to circulate. Yet some employees will refuse to share their knowledge or key data out of anger, jealousy, or insecurity.

One way to guard against such damaging behavior is to make sure several people are trained in specialized knowledge, such as advanced techniques that keep your computer systems running smoothly.

Companies often build redundancies into their computers systems to fall back on in an emergency, but they don't think of structuring their people resources that way. When they don't, the sole source of vital knowledge walks out the door at the end of her shift. Provide people backups; they make it harder for information hoarders to thrive.

Epilogue

Information hoarders are like a one-person relay team: Winning has value, teamwork doesn't.

21

Know When to Consult a Lawyer or Other Experts

Kevin, an office manager, was fed up with employees who quit without giving notice.

One woman called in her resignation two hours before she was supposed to report to work. He was so enraged that he crafted a policy to punish such irresponsible workers. Those workers would forfeit their final paycheck if they quit without giving a proper notice. But before adopting the policy he wrote me to ask if it was legal. Unfortunately, for him, it wasn't. Polices drafted out of anger usually are flawed. Kevin's proposal would violate labor laws. Hourly employees, which the woman was, have to be paid for all the time they work.

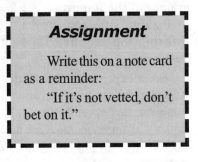

Assignment

Write this on a note card as a reminder:

"If it's not vetted, don't bet on it."

I suggested instead that he tie vacation eligibility to giving notice. Departing employees who are owed vacation time can claim it only if they give an acceptable notice. If you plan drastic changes in policy, vet them before you act. Consult a lawyer or other employment expert or the local office of the U.S. Department of Labor. If a wayward employee gives you a headache, unvetted corrective policies could give you migraines.

Epilogue

Before putting a new policy in place to take aim at problem employees, check with employment experts to make sure it's legal.

22

Don't Take Problem People Home

It is said that Einstein discovered a key element of his theory of relativity while at rest on a grassy knoll. Newton discovered the theory of gravity under an apple tree when a piece of the fruit fell and whacked him on the head. When it comes to problem-solving, taking a break from your problems is often the best strategy.

Give yourself a break from wrangling over personnel issues by not taking the problems home. If you have a flash of insight about how to better handle a difficult employee during dinner, write the idea down in a notebook and put it away until the following day.

Assignment

Indulge yourself at home. Do some crossword puzzles, play a board game, or just sink into an easy chair.

Ask yourself what you could possibly gain from fretting over an office problem at home. If the answer is nothing, that's all the more reason to set the problem aside until you return to work. Take the equivalent of a grassy-knoll break or apple-tree timeout. Let your time at home represent that. The clarity you'll gain could lead to a breakthrough.

Epilogue
Place the office baggage on the shelf at the end of the day.

41

23

When an Employee Threatens Violence

After Vernice Givens, who owns V&G Marketing Associates in Kansas City, fired an employee, the woman threatened her. She asked the woman to leave. Then Vernice and a security guard accompanied the agitated woman outside. Afterward, Vernice consulted an employment attorney about her next step.

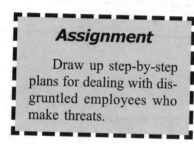

Assignment

Draw up step-by-step plans for dealing with disgruntled employees who make threats.

"Not only did I have to be concerned for my own safety, but that of my employees," she said.

She followed her attorney's advice and sent the woman a letter telling her that if she persisted, she would face legal action. That ended the problem.

Threats from employees are scary and should never be taken lightly. The appropriate action will depend on the circumstances and the employee, but you should assess the situation right away. Enlist the help of experts, if necessary, and formulate an appropriate response as soon as possible.

Epilogue

Better to be overly vigilant when it comes to workplace violence than to be caught off guard.

24

Offer Bullies Options, Not Just Objections

Workplace bullies are adults who never got over their "Terrible Twos," and just like those toddlers going through that unsettling phase of life, bullies believe they get what they want by acting out. When dealing with bully employees, your job as a leader is to show them more effective means for resolving conflict.

"Success and self-esteem are about knowing that you have choices," writes, Brian DesRoches in *Your Boss Is Not Your Mother: Creating autonomy, respect and success at work.* "Whenever you experience choices in how you relate with others, your ability to govern and direct your life is greatly enhanced."

If a bully is otherwise a valuable employee, then consider the options for

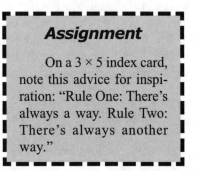

Assignment

On a 3 × 5 index card, note this advice for inspiration: "Rule One: There's always a way. Rule Two: There's always another way."

helping him or her. One way might be to require the employee to meet with an HR manager a few times to talk about anger management. If that's not doable, you could also insist that the employee attend a few outside sessions on non-violent communication, at the company's expense. Even when it comes to correcting a bully's behavior, the watchword is options.

> **Epilogue**
>
> *Bullies paint themselves and others into corners. Help them find a way out.*

25

Document Difficult Encounters

Leslie, manager at a fast-growing medical equipment company, laments that her company has retained so many people who are incompetent or defiant. The company is afraid of firing anyone because a couple of employees who were let go several years ago filed wrongful-termination lawsuits. The company was skittish—not because it thought the lawsuits had merit but because it lacked documentation about the employees' shortcomings. And it continued to give short shrift to that part of management to focus on its explosive growth.

> **Assignment**
>
> Create a special file to keep track of talks with a problem employee.

Without documentation, firings look fuzzy at best. They look downright suspicious when someone who won employee of the year is out the next because of a "poor performance" that isn't documented.

One of the first questions lawyers ask employers who seek advice on how to fire an incompetent employee is: "Did you document the problem?" If the answer is no, they will advise the employer to hold off until the documentation supports the decision.

Whether you are free to fire an employee doesn't matter.

What matters most is that you do your homework so the decision doesn't boomerang back to you.

Epilogue

If it bears repeating to an employee, write it down.

26

Monitor Phone Calls for Difficult Employees

I called a small-business owner for an interview. I got his name from a trade group that said he would be perfect for my story. Well, he might have been, except for his receptionist. When I called, she said he wasn't in. She didn't offer to take a message, but instead, she asked me to call back. She apparently didn't think the call was important enough to note. I passed on her boss. Some companies pay public relations people a lot of money to get exposure. That company could have gotten it free.

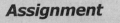

Assignment

Put together phone scripts that your employees should use as guidelines when speaking with customers.

Front-line employees, who deal with your customers wield enormous power. With a poor attitude, they turn off customers and cost you sales. Knowing how valuable calls are, some business owners ask friends and family to call their companies to gauge how employees handle calls. Be sure that your employees are helpful and courteous when customers call. And no one contacting the company during business hours should be instructed to call back. The employees should take a message and someone should return the call.

Make certain you have a policy to deal with workers who are belligerent or dismissive when handling phone calls. That way, a reprimand, transfer, or even dismissal won't seem arbitrary.

Epilogue

Your employees' good phone manners are like money in the bank for your business.

27

Acknowledge Employees for Defusing Tense Situations

You may have some people on your staff who excel in the role of peacemaker. When you hear of their heroic feats, praise them. They make your job of dealing with problem employees easier.

Oil magnate John D. Rockefeller knew the value of employees with extraordinary people skills:

"The ability to deal with people is as purchasable a commodity as sugar or coffee is, and I'll pay more for that ability than for any other under the sun."

If the natural mediators in your office break up a confrontation between warring colleagues or if they themselves exercise restraint when a colleague hurls insults at them, praise the peacemaker for displaying exemplary behavior. Say something such as, "I heard you handled that awful encounter well. Thank you."

These people are usually humble about their ability to keep the peace because negotiating skills come so naturally to them. And they, most likely, would continue their vital work without your praise. They still, however,

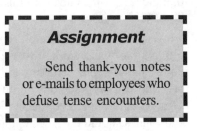

Assignment

Send thank-you notes or e-mails to employees who defuse tense encounters.

deserve recognition, especially in front of others who may be similarly inspired.

Epilogue

"No one is useless in this world who lightens the burdens of another."—Charles Dickens

28

The Office Isn't a Day Care

"Dad, how do I get an outside line to Washington again?" the young son of a coworker asked on his visit to the office. The son was visiting the office and spent a better part of the day making phone calls from a colleague's desk. The calls included several long-distance ones to Washington, D.C.

Assignment

Put together a policy for kid-visitors if you don't have one. Or if you have one, review it to make sure it works.

Most employees empathize with coworkers whose childcare arrangements break down at the last minute, leaving them with no option but to take their children to work. But people have no tolerance for colleagues who fail to supervise their children in the office.

Very few offices ban children. But too many lack policies to make the visits work. Just a few would help. You should require parents to accompany their children at all times. Visitors who use workstations should leave them as they found them. They should keep their voices down, and under no circumstances should they make long-distance calls without permission. You should also require parents to ask your permission to bring the kids to the office. If you agree, and if necessary, give the employee a copy of your visitors' policy.

Epilogue
When kids come to work, keep the office employee-friendly.

29

Use Irrational Requests as Conversational Openers

More than 75 percent of the obese people polled for a recent survey claimed they had healthy eating habits. And 40 percent said they exercised vigorously at least three times a week. The astounding responses, one doctor said, showed that the respondents were either ignorant or in denial about what constitutes a healthy diet or vigorous exercise.

Difficult employees often land in those zones of denial or ignorance. They have no clue about their shortcom-

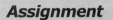

Assignment

Post a checklist of office perks available to employees in good standing. Include the eligibility criteria.

ings and, in fact, may hold themselves in much higher regard than you do. When they ask for special considerations such as a merit raise or the chance to work from home, consider that conversation your cue to remind her what the company expects from its employees. Tell the employee you will happily revisit her requests in a few months. But for now emphasize that you'd like her to focus on turning in the kind of performance that would put her in the running for office perks.

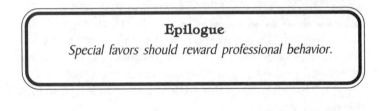

Epilogue
Special favors should reward professional behavior.

30

Hire Smart

One of the most striking things about the office of Dr. Jessica Jacob, who practices in New Hyde Park, New York, is its low staff turnover. Almost every assistant who was on staff when the doctor delivered my youngest son 13 years ago is still there.

They're not just hanging around to rack up seniority. They love what they do and it shows in how well they treat patients.

The doctor's secret is that she hires smart. She gives a lot of weight to an applicant's employment record.

"Generally if they have been elsewhere for a long time, that alone is a good sign."

She considers the first two weeks of employment a test period because "anyone can fool you on an interview." During this tryout phase, she gauges not only how competent her new hires are, but whether they work well with others, whether they take too many breaks, and whether they get to work on time.

> **Assignment**
>
> Create a list of interpersonal skills you look for in skilled applicants. Use it as checklist the next time you consider someone for a job.

"A late arrival in the first week or two, or a sick call, are horrible signs," she states. While talent is important, that shouldn't be the only factor you weigh when deciding to hire someone. You have to look at the total package if you want to avoid hiring a problem employee. That takes time. But it could take even longer to look for replacements.

Epilogue

When it comes to hiring smart, a prospect's competence is just the starting point.

31

Fire Smart

"Employers should always fire on the facts," an employment lawyer once told me. "You win a case based on the facts."

Yet too many employers are lulled into believing that they can forego documenting the facts if the company has the right to fire someone. While most state labor laws hold that employees who aren't covered by a contract can be fired at any time, that doesn't prevent wrongful termination lawsuits.

> ### *Assignment*
>
> If you think you may have to fire an employee, go over the paperwork you have to see if it supports your decision.

Your policies on what constitutes a fireable offense should be clear and distributed to employees. Your displeasure with a particular employee's work should come as no surprise to him when you call him in to deliver the bad news. Otherwise, the person could claim "ambush" and make your motives look suspicious.

"If you set the expectations at the beginning, and you are giving feedback, the employee will see the writing on the wall," said Diane Pfadenhauer, the owner of Employment Practices Advisors in Northport, New York.

If you provided the employee opportunities and resources to improve his performance, you certainly should document those good-faith efforts. That benevolence is proof that your intent wasn't to get rid of the person but to help him salvage a tarnished work record. It's hard to find fault with that.

Epilogue

Precede any firing with detailed documentation that justifies your action.

32

Encourage Employees to Tell You About Problem Colleagues

During my many years as an advice columnist, I've heard from concerned employees whose managers seemed afraid to talk to them. The supervisors, instead, spent a great deal of time holed up in their offices. By contrast I've witnessed the joy that employees feel when managers frequently ask them what's on their minds.

Assignment

Put out a suggestion box or establish an electronic one to encourage employees to communicate their ideas about how to use company resources better.

Your employees are intimately involved in your business and have valuable firsthand knowledge about how to improve it. That includes feedback on problem colleagues. Executives too busy to capitalize on that source of information are passing up invaluable opportunities. Jim Sinegal, the chief executive officer of the warehouse club, Costco, is legendary for his enthusiasm about communicating with his employees.

"The employees know I want to say hello to them because I like them," he said in an ABC News interview.

If you encourage open communication, your employees will alert you to a struggling colleague who needs your intervention. They may even have suggestions for improvement because they found themselves in similar circumstances. Let the helpful employees know you always welcome suggestions of how to put any of the company's resources to better use.

Epilogue

Often your own employees can provide the best ideas for improving a struggling colleague's work.

33

Don't Be Afraid to Critique Problem Managers

The perfect manager has never existed, yet some executives act as if the managers they hired are perfection itself. They take any criticism of these people personally, especially if the harsh words come from subordinates. And the execs are not above either ignoring the message or discrediting the messenger.

After Sherron Watkins, a vice president of Enron, complained about the dubious partnerships that high-ranking managers had created, she was made to feel like an outcast, according to some news reports. The company failed to take many of her recommendations seriously, recommendations that might have staved off Enron's meltdown.

Assignment

"Some managers need a good strong dose of their own medicine." Write that down on a 3 × 5 card as a reality check.

When a manager you hired or even mentored is accused of incompetence or malfeasance, don't take the complaint personally. Keep your eyes open to see if the complaints are worth giving serious consideration to.

Epilogue

Sometimes the problem employee is none other than a manager you hired. Handle that person as you would any employee with a similar problem.

34

When a Problem Employee Gives Notice

When my son broke his arm in two places, the best news I heard from the orthopedist was that they were "clean breaks." That meant no jagged edges, which are harder to set and take longer to heal.

In the workplace, managers pray for "clean breaks" when disgruntled employees give notice.

At that point, you have some tough questions to ask yourself? Does the risk of sabotage to equipment or projects loom large now that they have nothing riding on the job? If the answer is yes, you might want the employees to pack up and leave immediately. But if you do that, offer to pay them for the time they expected to stay after

Assignment

"Make every goodbye a clean break." Write that down on a 3 × 5 card and keep it handy for inspiration.

giving notice. You'll ensure the employees receive the final income they expected and you'll have peace of mind.

Some companies may balk at such payments as a form of extortion. But they wind up wasting time and money battling legal claims from tempestuous employees who are even more bad tempered because of the way their discharge was handled. The headache the owners thought they would be rid of as soon as the employees walked out the door returns with a vengeance.

If you take drastic measures to restore the office to normalcy after a difficult employees gives notice, make sure the strategy will work for all involved. Otherwise you will face a nasty break-up and an extended healing process.

Epilogue

When a difficult employee wants to exit the company, make sure the process of saying good-bye works for both of you.

35

Establish a System for Filing Complaints

The courts look favorably at companies that establish procedures for identifying and addressing employee complaints. The crafting of such policies reflects how serious the company is about tackling personnel conflicts, and that perception can make the difference between victory or defeat in a legal proceeding.

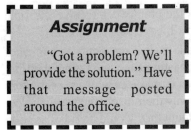

Assignment

"Got a problem? We'll provide the solution." Have that message posted around the office.

If your company is large enough, set up a hotline for those employees who want to tell you about an abusive manager or a sticky-fingered coworker but want to remain anonymous. Whether your business is small or large, designate someone like a human-resource manager or a supervisor to retrieve and follow through on the information, which should be kept confidential.

Formalized complaint procedures provide a system of checks and balances for unacceptable behavior. The systems can help you get at a problem before it gets you.

Epilogue

Make sure your company structure includes a formalized complaint system for employees.

36

Set an Example

It's hard to remain calm when dealing with an employee who makes the same mistakes over and over. Despite his promise to improve, the poor works continues. Out of sheer exasperation you want to resort to threats or turn up the volume to try to get through. If you take that route, however, you'll unwittingly set a negative tone for dealing with personnel problems. And your subordinates may follow your lead.

As a company leader you wield an awesome power that affects your employees' interpersonal skills. The example you set filters down through the ranks, contend the authors of *Conquer Your Critical Inner Voice.*

"In general, workers adopt the same attitudes and behaviors in their interactions with coworkers and customers that their employer displays toward them."

Assignment

If you mishandled a personnel problem in a less than exemplary way, try to figure out what went wrong.

As the saying goes, "Imitation is the sincerest form of flattery." Make sure you always exhibit behavior you'd be proud to have your employees imitate.

Epilogue

Make sure your solutions for problem employees don't create larger problems for you.

37

Encourage Managers to Communicate Problems Up the Chain

When the school year starts, I make a point to introduce myself to my high schoolers' teachers. I ask them to keep me

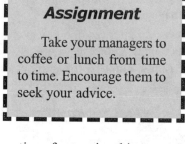

Assignment

Take your managers to coffee or lunch from time to time. Encourage them to seek your advice.

apprised of any problems with my teenagers' work. I also keep in touch throughout the school year. I make the effort because I don't want to be surprised by any problems at the end of the school year, when students have fewer options for turning things around.

As a manager, major problems, especially personnel problems, shouldn't catch you by surprise. An open revolt of the staff or the resignation of a star player shouldn't be the first time you hear about an ongoing problem on your staff.

Make it clear to your managers that, while you have faith in their abilities to handle their subordinates' problems, you want to be informed about the egregious ones. So, occasionally, ask your managers if they are facing any difficult personnel issues and how they're handling them. Assure them that when they're at their wits' end it's okay to ask for your advice.

Epilogue
Insist on updates about difficult personnel issues.

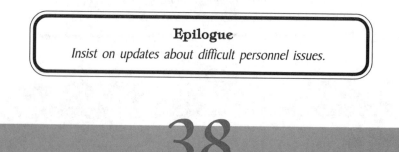

No Across-the-Board Reprimands

A manager bent on impressing his bosses decided he'd punish wastrels by removing paper towels from the company's restrooms. Without preparing the staff, he removed paper towel dispensers and installed hand dryers. After the fact, he explained that some employees had wasted too much paper. With dryers, his argument went, the company would save on paper and cleaning costs.

The decision was a dismal failure. In his zeal to punish all for the sins of a few,

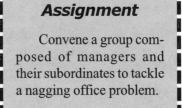

Assignment

Convene a group composed of managers and their subordinates to tackle a nagging office problem.

the manager didn't think about the consequences of his actions. Employees had no towels to clean up coffee spills or to wipe spots from their clothes. Howls of protest went up. The manager reversed himself and restored the paper towels.

Employees seldom buy into broad-brush solutions to a problem. The approach feels more like punishment than a solution.

Always try to tailor your message to the problem. If some employees are wasteful, focus your message to them. Hang up a sign reminding them to not waste paper. You'd probably be surprised at their willingness to cooperate.

Epilogue

One-size-fits-all remedies seldom prove effective in the long run.

39

Don't Parent a Difficult Employee

It's easy to find yourself falling into the parent trap at work. You may feel a great affinity for a young, ambitious employee because he attended your alma mater. And the person's charisma and big ideas may wow you. So when he refuses to do an assignment he considers beneath him you may just let him have his way. You may tell his supervisor to find something more worthy of your protégé's talent. If you do, you're parenting, not leading.

> **Assignment**
>
> Make sure the so-called grunt work is evenly distributed.

Jason was chomping at the bit to move into management. He had become chummy with a high-ranking executive who was impressed with his Ivy League background and superb organizational skills. Jason's boss, a middle manager, asked him to take on a project. Even though Jason was relatively new to the company, he considered the work beneath him. He felt the assignment would slow down his march to management. He complained to his mentor, the executive, and he, in turn, asked the manager to assign the project to someone else. The co-worker who inherited the assignment felt dumped on.

If an employee is so special that should mean he could take on any assignment and produce good work. Sure you have to challenge bright employees with plum assignments, but they shouldn't be shielded from work that everyone else is expected to tackle. If you find yourself frequently going out of normal channels to accommodate a demanding would-be star, you're acting more like Daddy than Manager.

Epilogue

Don't parent; lead.

40

Audit Teams for Hot Spots

Talent matters on a team. But in many respects, teamwork matters more. Former Los Angeles Lakers teammates Kobe Bryant and Shaquille O'Neal illustrate famously how talent minus teamwork equals a losing team. While the two superstars feuded, the team failed to win an NBA final. Once coach Phil Jackson put an end to the fighting, the pair led the Lakers to three championships. "Teams do only as well as the team leader," says Joanne Sujansky, president of the Key Group, a Pittsburgh workplace-consulting group. When team members' work falters, the leader should take responsibility for making them perform better, Sujansky says. The leader should motivate, set standards and offer coaching. Most importantly the leader should find out why the member's productivity slipped.

> ### Assignment
>
> "Hot heads and cold hearts never solved anything."—Rev. Billy Graham. Use that quote as part of your pep talk to a team.

"We might learn something and be able to guide that person to be a better performer," she says.

Fully functioning teams are invaluable to any organization, but, as the NBA superstars showed, that value can easily slip away when un-team like attitudes take hold.

Epilogue
A winning team knows the value of real teamwork.

41

Remove a Team Member if Necessary

Vernice Givens, the owner of a Kansas City marketing firm, asked her assistant to put together the first draft of a brochure that would be included among the company's hand-out literature. After completing the draft, the woman was supposed to circulate it among her teammates for com-

Assignment

If you dread removing a team member, ask yourself if you would fire yourself if you performed in similar fashion. If the answer is a resounding "Yes," you should act.

ments, but the woman waited until the last minute to write the initial draft. Her teammates then had to rush through it to meet the next deadline. That perpetuated a chain of events that resulted in an inferior first effort. It was not the first time. Vernice had repeatedly talked with the woman about the importance of pacing herself for complex tasks. But the overconfident woman repeatedly neglected big assignments until the 11th hour. That coupled with other problems prompted Vernice to show her the door.

If an employee fails to improve after you've coached her or assigned her to a more suitable project, then you have to consider removing the person from the team or firing her, says Joanne Sujansky, founder and president of the Key Group, a Pittsburgh workplace-consulting group.

If you retain the underperformer too long, she says, you risk demoralizing other team members, hurting productivity, and worse for you, making you look like a weak manager.

Epilogue

When team members don't pull their weight on a team, they're weighing it down and may have to go.

42

Mine the Exit Interviews

Exit interviews provide an excellent opportunity for identifying and dealing with difficult employees. In general, many companies consider information from exit interviews important. Seventy-six percent of the executives surveyed in a recent poll by the staffing company OfficeTeam said they acted on information gathered during exist interviews.

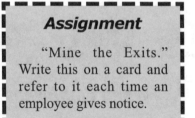

Assignment

"Mine the Exits." Write this on a card and refer to it each time an employee gives notice.

Departing employees, particularly those who have lined up a job elsewhere, will most likely be honest about their difficult coworkers and how you handled them.

Try to find out what you could have done to make their working life more pleasant. The person may be hostile if she feels she was driven away by a tyrant or a bully, but pick through the discussion for useful information. And use the information as a starting point for discussions with the problem manager or coworker.

After a particularly revealing exit interview, conduct what experts call the "stay interview," with employees you want to hang onto. Try to determine if they share any of a departing colleague's concerns about troubling coworkers and supervisors. If so, find out what they need from you and assure them you intend to handle their concerns as quickly as possible.

Epilogue

When you mine an exit interview you use the end of one relationship to build on others.

43

When Employees Resist Change

Employees fight change when they fear it. During the Industrial Revolution in Britain, the infamous Luddites feared losing their jobs to textile machines, so the workers destroyed the equipment.

"Change, not habit, is what gets most of us down," said William Feather. The most memorable companies I have worked for recognized the uneasiness change could cause employees. One employer understood the potential for high-stress among employees when it considered replacing its computers. Employees would quickly go from masters of one system to novices of another.

> **Assignment**
>
> Break down the phases of a planned change. Brainstorm with a committee on how to offer support.

The company supported us through every phase of the proposed change. It asked employees to serve on a committee that would choose a system. It issued memos about upcoming changes well in advance. It provided training and materials. Once the system was in use, it asked employees to alert their supervisors to any difficulties. It didn't assume employees would embrace the change. It simply made it easier to do so.

Like anything else in business, change is a process. If you provide employees support along the way, you will lower their resistance to it.

Epilogue

"In times of rapid change, experience could be your worst enemy."—John Paul Getty

---

44

Nix Managers' Gossip About Employees

Some managers excel at missing opportunities, especially when the opportunity involves staff development. I've worked for managers who complained to everyone about under-performing employees except the employee himself. Once, when I was speaking with a manager in his office, he took a call from coworker notorious for turning in reports that were late and long. After their tense discussion, the manager slammed down the phone and said, right in front of me, "I wish he would quit."

That kind of talk is wrong on so many levels. First of all it doesn't help the employee in question improve his or her performance. Secondly, that kind of talk makes other employees wonder what managers say about them.

When remarks like that come to you attention, ask the manager three questions:

Have you told the employee about the problem? If not, why not? Have you worked out a plan for improvement? Those questions will help shift the focus of the manager's conversations about his employees' performance to staff development, where it should be.

Epilogue

Ask the supervisor of a struggling employee about a plan for improvement.

45

The Greatest No-Shows on Earth

Because the Fourth of July fell on a Tuesday in 2006, I was asked to write a story about whether many companies planned to close the Monday before to give their employees a long week-end. If they weren't planning to grant the bridge day, I asked if they were bracing for no-shows. To one office manager the question seemed strange.

"We are a close-knit group and we would never do that to one another," she said. Some companies would kill for that kind of worker camaraderie, especially if it prevents no-shows. Instead, many employers find themselves waging a costly war with absenteeism. The business-research company CCH estimates that unscheduled, paid absences cost some large companies close to $1 million a year. Yet just 35 percent of employees absences involve illness, CCH says.

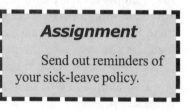

Assignment

Send out reminders of your sick-leave policy.

If you're a small-business owner you know how just one unexpected absence can throw your staffing situation into turmoil. As soon as you suspect someone is abusing your sick-leave policy, share with them the hardship the office faces when employees fail to show up for work. Ask if a later start or other accommodation would help the person make it to work and make it clear that sick days are for the sick.

Epilogue

Unexpected absences wreak havoc on the frontlines and the bottom line.

Is the Work Load Balanced?

It's no secret that today's workers typically face heavier workloads and longer hours. In fact, some companies have shifted into the inverse mode of trying to do more work with fewer employees. Despite this dire imbalance, many offices still have workers who successfully fight off attempts to ask them to do more. In the face of their fierce resistance, some managers simply take the path of least resistance and add to the in-basket of their more agreeable workers.

That approach will keep the less industrious happy, but will also breed resentment among the overworked on your staff. Now more than ever, it is imperative that you even out the workloads. If the amount of work requires your employees to spend more time in the office, the least you can do is make sure everyone is pitching in.

> **Assignment**
>
> Make note of this quote by Sir Walter Bilbey: "The employer generally gets the employees he deserves."

Don't wait for workers to come to you to complain about unequal workloads. Go on the offensive. Put out a memo making it clear that you can't or won't tolerate the workload inequities and that you expect everyone to do what is asked of them. It won't lighten the workload overall but it will keep resentment from working overtime.

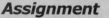

Epilogue

The success of your business depends on all your employees rising to the challenge each day.

47

Don't Undercut Your Managers

When Josh agreed to take over a temporary supervisory position, the department head told him to lean on a star salesman to submit his expense reports on time. The salesman was notoriously late, and the finance office would complain to the department head. The same week Josh got his marching orders, he called the salesman and urged him to make every effort to comply. The day before the expenses were due he phoned him again and reminded him of the deadline. The salesman hung up the phone in a huff and complained to the boss that Josh was too pushy. The boss told Josh to ease up. Josh gave up.

Your blessing is the best thing your managers have going into a conversation with a problem worker. If the problem employee senses a rupture in your unity, he or she will try to capitalize on

Assignment

If one of your managers has a meeting with a troublemaker, drop in to lend your support to the supervisor.

that. When you undercut your managers, you simply enable difficult employees.

Epilogue

If you entrust your managers with a plan, back them up in the execution of it.

48

Don't Forget About Your Other Employees

Difficult employees in some sense are like the squeaky wheel. They get the oil, or in their case, the attention. You may focus so much on resolving their issues that you forget you are

---
Assignment

When you're battling with a troublemaker, thank a staffer who has performed well.

---

the leader of the entire office. Even if you eventually dismiss the problem employee, you want to keep the office functioning as normally as possible until you do. During those trying times, it helps to remind yourself of your responsibilities to the rest of the staff. You should always strive to:

- ◆ Create an environment in which productivity and creativity thrive.
- ◆ Be a fierce guardian of employee morale.
- ◆ Show your appreciation for good work.

- ◆ Show your gratitude for self-starters.
- ◆ Thank employees who go the extra mile in turbulent times.
- ◆ Create a workplace known for fairness.

Some employees are so low maintenance they are easy to take for granted. Make sure you avoid that.

Epilogue

Although difficult employees' problems put them front and center, they aren't your only constituents.

49

Help! How to Find an Attorney

Before mountaineers brave the treacherous trek up Mt. Everest they enlist the aid of local Sherpa. They're the experienced guides who help the climbers survive the punishing slopes and deep crevasses.

When the office terrain turns bleak because of personnel problems, you may need a lawyer to function as your Sherpa. If you want to fire someone you suspect of stealing or feel a manager needs sexual-harassment training, you should consult an attorney.

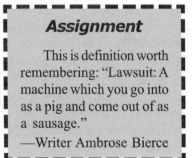

Assignment

This is definition worth remembering: "Lawsuit: A machine which you go into as a pig and come out of as a sausage."

—Writer Ambrose Bierce

The best way to find a lawyer is the same way to find any good expert: referrals. Ask other business owners for recommendations. Steven D. Strauss, the author of *The Small Business Bible: Everything you need to know to succeed in your small business*, suggests that you ask the referring client probing questions. Inquire if the lawyer got good results, if the attorney was accessible, if the fees were reasonable, and who does the work, the attorney or less-experienced associates. When you feel you've run out of options, or are unsure of the legality of your options, it's good to have a good lawyer on your conflict-resolution team.

Epilogue
Before you begin a trek, find a guide.

Refer to EAP

Some personnel problems will simply exceed your ability to handle them, but if you want to hold onto an employee minus his or her destructive behavior, an Employee Assistance Program (EAP) is a good next step. When you provide your employees with this benefit, you give them access to expert counseling that is confidential.

"The intention is to save a good employee and allow them to save face in the process," says John Putzier, an industrial psychologist and president of FirStep Inc., a consulting firm in Prospect, Pennsylvania.

Ask your human-resource department to handle the referral to EAP since they are usually trained to handle personnel matters, Putzier says. If you don't have an HR department, then designate a supervisor. But make it clear that confidentiality is a priority.

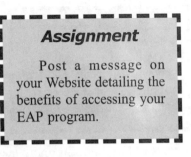

Assignment

Post a message on your Website detailing the benefits of accessing your EAP program.

When you broach the topic of counseling with the employee keep the conversation tightly focused on how the person's work is suffering because of the behavior. That's the very reason you want them to get help.

"It starts with the performance," Putzier says. "If there isn't a performance issue it's technically none of your business."

Epilogue

Add an EAP benefit to your tool kit for dealing with problem employees.

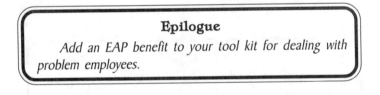

51

Give Yourself a Break

Many companies give their employees breaks because they know it's important for them to rest their bodies and their minds.

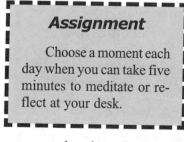

Assignment

Choose a moment each day when you can take five minutes to meditate or reflect at your desk.

Give yourself breaks, too, to help balance a particularly trying day of personnel conflicts with some worry-free time for yourself.

Rest during the day is a hard concept for hard-charging small-business owners to buy into. So many take better care of their businesses than themselves.

"Some of us get so used to operating in a state of anxiety that just trying to relax can create anxiety," write Jim Claitor and Colleen Contreras in *Build the Life You Want and Still Have Time to Enjoy It*.

Take a cue from some executives who lead major corporations. Go to your office, turn off the lights, and put your head down for a few minutes. Give yourself a 15-minute holiday of pure nothingness. Give up your problems (temporarily) so you won't give out.

Epilogue

Sometimes the best way to deal with static is to turn off the TV.

Put an End to Pilfering

A bookkeeper hooked on lottery tickets pleaded guilty to embezzling $2.3 million from a medical office. She was able to help herself to her bosses' money for more than three years because she was the sole keeper of the books.

It's not uncommon for a single person to handle key operations at small businesses. That's why they're easy prey for in-house

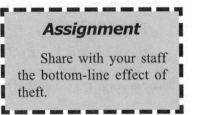

Assignment

Share with your staff the bottom-line effect of theft.

thieves. The owners are often too trusting or too busy running their businesses to give anti-theft measures a priority. While most employees are honest, it's paramount you make sure your business isn't vulnerable to those who aren't.

The U.S Small Business Administration suggests a few simple measures: Divide key tasks such as inventory and book-keeping among several staff members. Establish an employee-awareness program to help your employees help you detect theft, and formulate a clear policy about the crime and the punishment.

Whatever measures you take, consider them as mere supplements to good-old fashioned vigilance.

Epilogue

You should never let trust cancel out vigilance.

53

Vary Your Tactics

Sometimes a supervisor's answer to entrenched personnel problems is surrender. That creates a class of employees the company VitalSmarts calls "untouchables." In a recent

Assignment

Use this quote for inspiration: "Where there is an open mind, there will always be a frontier."
—Inventor Charles Kettering

poll, the training company found that 93 percent of employees work with an "untouchable." These are colleagues who are able to retain their jobs despite their bad behavior or underperformance.

In tightly run companies, an underperforming product is repositioned or dropped. If you're not yet ready to cut your losses with an underperformer or a bully, then you have to keep working with the employee until the problem goes away. Otherwise, you'll send the message that mediocrity is tolerated. If stern talks didn't nudge the employee to meet deadlines or if forcing him to keep a work log doesn't help, maybe pairing the person with a mentor will make the problem disappear. The answer is out there and until it's "You're fired," you have to keep searching for it.

Epilogue

Just like business plans, strategies for dealing with employees sometimes need revamping.

54

Suggest Better Work Habits

If a fairy godmother could grant 25-hour days, some people would probably fritter away the extra hour. The average

American worker squanders two hours of an eight-hour workday, according to an AOL/ *Salary.Com* survey. That's about twice what employers expected. And that nonproductive time doesn't even include lunch or breaks.

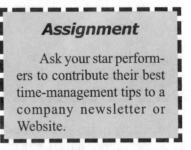

Assignment

Ask your star performers to contribute their best time-management tips to a company newsletter or Website.

Some employees have a difficult time with time management, and they aren't going to improve until you help them. You're probably in a good position to do so because many entrepreneurs are excellent time managers. They have to be. Give procrastinators hints of how they can parse a project into manageable pieces and determine how much time they'll need for each phase. That's also an excellent strategy for helping them to envision how a project unfolds from the present into the future. Time then becomes something they can see. And it ceases to become a shapeless mass that mysteriously slips away each day.

Epilogue
Invest in your employees by offering time-management skills regularly.

55

Send Employees for More Training

Many companies talk about the importance of good customer service. But far too many fail to let their employees in on the secret. Rude employees too often are the first point of contact for customers.

Assignment

Bring in a customer-service trainer for a day.

Have your relatives test your customer service. You may not like the feedback. And you may have to admit that your employees need retraining to take your customer service to a higher level. Some banks and car dealerships eager to spiff up their customer service have sent their employees to boot camps offered by luxury hotels noted for stellar service, according to the *Wall Street Journal*.

Your employees may need some outside training, too. Customer service won't substitute for a great product, but it will help get more of a great product into customers' hands.

Epilogue
You have to make good customer service happen.

56

No Knee-Jerk Reactions

Psychologists divide our interactions into two broad categories: responses and reactions. A response is a deliberate, well thought-out action. A reaction is knee-jerk and lacking in thought and insight. A reaction generates regrets, not solutions. Hurling insults at an offending employee is knee-jerk. Reminding him that you expect professional behavior at all times is a response.

A reaction reinforces the status quo. A response is a change agent and provides insight.

"The best vision is insight," said magazine publisher and entrepreneur Malcolm Forbes.

So slow down, take a deep breath and respond, not react.

Assignment

Play back some difficult encounters with employees in your mind. See how you could have responded rather than reacted.

Epilogue

You'll leave a lasting impression if you respond to a problem rather than react to it.

57

Is the Affair Bad for Business?

A tee-totaling boss wanted to prohibit her employees from drinking on business trips, even after work. She wrote to ask if such a policy was legal. It's risky because some states have laws that prohibit employers from intruding on their employees' lives after hours.

But what goes on in your office is another matter. The

Assignment

Include discussions about the drawbacks of extramarital affairs in sensitivity-training for managers.

primary consideration regarding any behavior you deem unacceptable is whether it interferes with business. Two single colleagues who date may not be a concern, but a manager who has an affair with a subordinate, especially an extramarital one, might prove a costly distraction in the office. He will be the target of constant gossip and employees will view anything he does for his paramour as favoritism. The girlfriend, if jilted, could become angry enough to accuse the manager of sexual harassment.

Even if you don't have a policy against dating—and 90 percent of companies don't according to the online jobsite, *Vault.com*—you have to act before a relationship interferes with business.

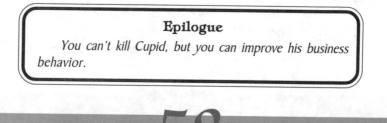

Epilogue

You can't kill Cupid, but you can improve his business behavior.

58

Handling the Nasty End to Subordinates' Romance

A messy break-up can make difficult employees out of some of the most professional people. A once-happy couple may declare all-out war on each other in the office and you'll have to mediate. Keep your role simple. Remind them both of the office's code of conduct. If the ex-lovers put on public spectacles worthy of the Jerry Springer show, remind them both that you won't tolerate unprofessional behavior. But be as compassionate as you can, because a break-up is akin to grieving. You, however, still have

> **Assignment**
>
> Redistribute your code of conduct to employees who date when it seems appropriate.

to run a business and don't want distractions from a soured romance.

If the couple are both good workers and you want to retain them, you may have to take the drastic step of removing both of them from a team. Treat each employee equally. Don't take sides. One half of the couple may try to force you into that role, but don't take the bait.

> **Epilogue**
>
> *No one's personal problems should overtake your business.*

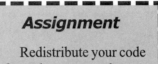

59

Addressing an Employee Who Won't Dress the Part

Some companies have attempted to give employees more wardrobe freedom with "Casual Fridays," but some

Assignment

Have an image consultant come in and offer employees tips on how to dress professionally. Make attendance voluntary.

employees became so lax that their companies canceled that exercise in relative sartorial freedom.

Nationwide Insurance recently revised its dress code to ban midriff-baring tops, T-shirts, and flip-flops, according to the *Wall Street Journal*. Another large national insurance company has tightened up its dress code so much that even customer-service employees who never come face to face with the public aren't allowed to wear sneakers on the job.

You have a right to demand that employees dress to reflect a professional environment, and your expectations should be written in a code of conduct and distributed to employees. Violations and responses should be spelled out. You should avoid extreme demands that would violate the civil rights of employees who dress in accordance with their religion or culture. Even so, you'll still have a lot of leeway to get your employees to look like the professionals they are supposed to be.

Epilogue
Make sure your office image isn't hanging by a thread.

60

A Wake-Up Call for Stragglers

I belong to a meditation group with exemplary time-management skills. The sittings always start promptly at 8 a.m. Latecomers have to cool their heels in the hall until the group files out for a walking meditation. That's Zen and the no-nonsense approach to meetings.

Employees who repeatedly show up late for meetings should always

Assignment

Make a habit of starting and ending meetings on time.

find a meeting in progress, not one awaiting their arrival. They shouldn't be rewarded with a recap of what they missed. If they are scheduled to speak at the top of the meeting, proceed to the next item on the agenda. When the stragglers arrive make them cool their heels, if necessary, until you can fit in their presentation. The embarrassment of such awkwardness eventually may be just the wake-up call the straggler needs.

Epilogue

Meeting start times should never begin with a straggler.

61

Use an Evaluation as a Blueprint for Transforming Problem Employees

Early in my career, I worked for a company with a simple rule for evaluations: Supervisors couldn't use an evaluation to bring up performance issues for the first time. That rule made the assessment seem less like an attack and more like a framework for improvement.

Assignment

Have your HR department put together a half-day seminar on how to write evaluations or arrange for a trainer to come in.

Far too many supervisors use evaluations as a weapon to get back at problem employees. The frustration is understandable, but the simple truth is that supervisors who use evaluations primarily to upbraid employees violate sound business practices. An evaluation should inspire employees to improve.

Allow employees to respond to their evaluations. Read your managers' assessments. Then read their subordinates.' If you suspect the manager is using the evaluation as a reprisal, remind him or her of the purpose of an evaluation.

Epilogue
An evaluation shouldn't bring up something an employee hasn't already heard.

Call Employees on Inappropriate Computer and Internet Use

In just one week, 7,700 workers at the U.S. Department of the Interior made more than one million visits to gaming and auction sites, despite a ban on such activity. The time spent on the sites factored out to 2,000 hours of lost productivity in a single week and a potential of more than 100,000 hours a year, according to a federal report that detailed the abuse.

The findings are potent reminders of the double-edged sword the Internet has become. It enhances work, but it also detracts from it.

Make sure your policy makes clear how employees put your business at risk when they visit unauthorized sites during work and what the consequences are. Your company could be sued for sexual harassment. Or it could be thrust into the public eye because an employee used the company computer to access kiddy porn.

Assignment

From time to time, post articles on the company bulletin board about the high cost of abusive Internet use.

Some employers ban non-business uses of the computer all together, even during lunchtime. Others allow "discrete" use. Craft a policy that makes sense for your office. You shouldn't punish the whole office because of a few bad apples. Enlist the help of your information-technology staff or hire a specialist to monitor your system for policy violations.

Epilogue

Keep Internet abusers in the hot seat with a policy and enforcement of it.

63

Nip Managers' Favoritism in the Bud

Favoritism often leads to the wrong people for the job, sometimes with tragic consequences. Michael Brown, the former director of the Federal Emergency Management Agency, had little emergency-management experience when he took over the reins of the agency. His predecessor, who is also a longtime friend, recommended him for the job. Brown resigned following fierce criticism about FEMA's relief efforts in the aftermath of Hurricane Katrina.

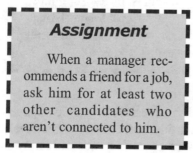

Assignment

When a manager recommends a friend for a job, ask him for at least two other candidates who aren't connected to him.

Your managers may be eager to surround themselves with loyal employees or longtime friends. Nothing is inherently wrong with that plan as long as it furthers your business objective to find the best person for the job. But if the narrow views thwart your attempts to bring diversity into your office and to find the most qualified people, tell the managers to cast a wider net. When they recommend candidates, evaluate the choices and compare them with others who have interviewed for the job. Always lean more toward talent than familiarity.

Epilogue

Make sure favoritism doesn't corrupt your hiring process.

64

Remove Abusive Managers

Executives with a vision have clear objectives. They also have clear ideas about what kind of managers they want to carry out those objectives.

Soon after a manager took over a department at a large communications company, she interviewed all the employees to determine their concerns. The name of a difficult supervisor surfaced again and again. The woman was known for

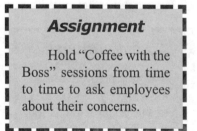

Assignment

Hold "Coffee with the Boss" sessions from time to time to ask employees about their concerns.

sabotage. When angry, she frequently walked out and left her work for others to do. She forced people to attend meetings on her behalf without briefing them. She constantly blamed others for her mistakes.

Shortly after all the interviews, the department head removed the woman to a non-managerial position, much to the delight of those who had worked for her.

An abusive manager can unleash a plague of ills in your office: Absenteeism, low-productivity, increased turnover, and smoldering resentment. Reassign them or cut them loose.

Epilogue

Inventorying your business should also involve taking stock of your managers.

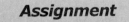

When Employees Ask to Borrow Money

An employee borrowed several thousand dollars from her boss. He agreed to take $50 out of her check every two weeks. But he soon grew impatient with that rate of repayment. On his own, he later decided to take out as much as $600 each pay period. Upset, the woman

Assignment

If an employee asks to borrow money, say no to a loan but yes to referrals for banks with the best loan rates.

asked me if that huge deduction was legal. It wasn't. In many states employers must request employees' written permission for deductions—except for taxes.

Even though her employer's initial intentions were good, his frustrations got the best of him. To the employee he went from friendly banker to robber baron and she planned to take legal action. Both employee and employer should have heeded the time-honored advice: "Neither a borrower nor lender be."

Epilogue

Making loans to employees shouldn't be part of any business plan.

66

Why an Apology Matters

"Round up the usual suspects." That line from the beloved movie *Casablanca* is sometimes the strategy managers rely on to deal with difficult employees. It's easy to assume they are always at fault when something goes wrong because they are often at fault. Sometimes you will err, though, and when you do, apologize.

In *The 7 Habits of Highly Effective People*, management guru Stephen Covey labels such mistakes as "withdrawals from the Emotional Bank Account." They can often be reversed with a simple apology.

Assignment

"Courage is grace under pressure." Write this Hemingway quote on 3 × 5 card to use for inspiration.

"When we make withdrawals from the Emotional Bank Account, we need to apologize and we need to do it sincerely," he writes, "Great deposits come in the sincere words: 'I was wrong....'"

Too many managers subscribe to the notion that you should never apologize, especially to a problem employee. They mistakenly believe it makes them look weak.

In fact, the opposite is true. It takes great courage. If you don't muster that courage, you create an even bigger problem for yourself. You may undercut the self-esteem of the employee who was trying to improve. He may simply ask himself, "What's the use?"

Epilogue

An apology gives you yet another opportunity to embody your values.

67

Remind Employees of the Chain of Command

A chain of command is important in business. It allows executives to determine who should be held accountable for a personnel problem. To insubordinate employees, though, a chain of command means nothing. They flout authority, after all. They won't hesitate to leapfrog over their supervisor to take their concerns to the very top. Their approach could leave their supervisor feeling diminished.

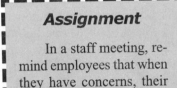

Assignment

In a staff meeting, remind employees that when they have concerns, their supervisor should be their first point of contact.

If an employee breaks protocol and comes directly to you with an issue, remind the person of the chain of command with two questions: (1) Did you speak with your supervisor? (2) What was the outcome?

A chain of command shouldn't be too rigid, though. If an employee's immediate supervisor is abusive or ineffective, the employee should by all means be encouraged to jump up the chain to find relief.

Epilogue
Don't allow insubordinate employees to rearrange your chain of command.

68

Demand Sensitivity Training

A woman who wrote me had the misfortune of working with the Boss from Yell. The manager, a disorganized workaholic, yelled at employees when they couldn't stay late. She yelled at them when they asked for help. She yelled to get their attention. Yelling was her idea of staff development.

The insensitive behavior drove people away, yet it didn't faze her. She wore the departures like badges of honor: "See. I don't have to fire them. I'm good at making them quit."

> **Assignment**
>
> Use this quote as a reality check when dealing with a bully manager: "The angry man always thinks he can do more than he can."
> —Albertano de Brescia

She apparently has a lot of company. In a recent Gallup poll of one million workers, a bad boss was the Number-1 reason cited for leaving a job. If you see a manager churning through employees, don't just buy the line that good help is hard to find. Hold staff meetings to air concerns and take some of the managers' subordinates to lunch to find out what is going on in their division. If you agree that the manager is a problem, then order her to take an anger-management course or other sensitivity training. If you take the time to find good people, the last thing you want is a manager who nullifies those good efforts.

Epilogue

A manager should manage, not intimidate and humiliate.

69

By the Way, "This Is Your Job"

One of the most damning statements an employee could utter is "It's not my job." That's an employee who is totally disengaged from a company. People who take that stance won't go out of their way to answer a phone or help a customer. They're too busy deciding what they won't do.

One way to head off such productivity-killing declarations is to make sure you give employees a written description of their jobs. Conscientious employees will always pitch in. But for less cooperative types, you need to spell out what you need from them. If you need employees who aren't clerks to occasionally answer the phone, put that

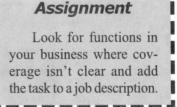

Assignment

Look for functions in your business where coverage isn't clear and add the task to a job description.

in the description. If you need them to stay a few minutes longer on some days to help take care of late customers, then say that. Pay them for the extra time. Too many companies create the "It's-not-my-job types" by sneaking in extra work without paying employees for the time. Otherwise, even the most loyal employees will start to gripe.

Review the job descriptions frequently and change them to reflect any extra duties an employee has taken on. A solid job description keeps both you and your employees honest about what a job really entails. It will give you the confidence to say, "Yes, it is your job."

Epilogue
If you want a job done, put it in a job description.

70

Don't Be Star Struck

Star employees are tricky beings. They can make your business, but, unrestrained, they can also be its undoing. Star managers were credited with Enron's explosive growth. However, they were also responsible for the company's demise.

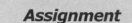

Assignment

When you evaluate star employees, rate them on interpersonal interactions as well.

You may unknowingly bestow a "halo" on your star players. That is, you will assume that because their sales record is impeccable, all other aspects of their work are perfect as well. And because you are so convinced of their flawlessness, you may discount any complaints about them. For their part, the star players may assume that the hands-off treatment means they are above the usual workplace policies.

Unrestrained stars may be abusive to coworkers. Or they may set their own hours and days off, without any regard for the office's staffing needs.

The best way to rein in the office "royals" it to hold them to the same rules as you would "the commoners." Reward the star for her fine work but remind her that while she may be in a class by herself when it comes to her performance, she isn't when it comes to the company code of conduct.

Epilogue

Arrogance and entitlement never wear well in business.

71

Know When to Cut Your Losses

Saying good-bye is hard. But greeting an employee, day in and day out, who just can't cut it is even harder. It's a reminder that you are paying for incompetence.

No matter how much potential some employees seem to possess or how much help you've given them, they still produce substandard work. The longer you wait to cut them loose, the more your motives will be ques-

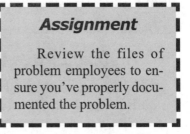

Assignment

Review the files of problem employees to ensure you've properly documented the problem.

tioned. Then you'll have to answer questions like, "After all these years, why is my work suddenly a problem?"

And if you haven't communicated the employee's failings clearly or if you lack documentation, firing them will seem arbitrary. After all, incompetent people are often the last to recognize their shortcomings.

Former General Electric chairman and CEO Jack Welch put it bluntly in a news story, "As long as the turkeys aren't being told they're turkeys, they don't mind being there."

But how can you tell when you've really reached the point of no return? Listen to your gut and look to your paper trail. It they are in synch, then it's time to act.

If your aim is to assemble a highly qualified staff, you'll have to say goodbye to a few liabilities to make room for more assets.

Epilogue

Never rush to dismiss a struggling employee. But once you've made up your mind, act.

72

Discourage Workaholics

The dictionary defines a workaholic as "one who has a compulsive and unrelenting need to work." Some, workaholics, though, are simply horrible time managers. They sometimes keep long hours because they squander huge blocks of time during the height of the workday. They take long lunches or socialize for hours. They then rally to make up that time by staying after hours to finish work they could have completed earlier. If someone needs a report from them during business hours, workaholics stave them off with stories of how overwhelmed they are and how late they have to work to keep up with the workload. They're simply suffering from inefficiency hangovers.

> **Assignment**
>
> Require all employees to get permission before working extra hours.

Don't indulge workaholics, especially if you're unsure why they put in such long hours. Insist that they adhere to the company schedule, particularly if you have to pay them for the extra hours. Most importantly, make sure you show by example that efficiency and a work/life balance beat workaholism any day.

Epilogue
Workaholics don't always have your best business interest at heart.

73

What's in It for Me?

Modern-day business lore has its share of stories about fanatical cost-cutters who so excelled at laying off employees that the eliminator's job became redundant and met with the ax as well.

Anybody can cut staff and the cuts don't always have the expected outcome. But it takes talent and vision to grow a company. That process begins with your staff. Sure you can continually dismiss problematic employees. As an alternative, though, you could invest in them until you consider them utterly unsalvageable. Why should you? When you invest in any of your staff you increase their chances for success and by extension yours. What's more, if you know how to develop employees, you're way ahead of a lot of companies.

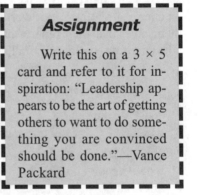

Assignment

Write this on a 3 × 5 card and refer to it for inspiration: "Leadership appears to be the art of getting others to want to do something you are convinced should be done."—Vance Packard

Wegmans, a Rochester, New York-based supermarket chain legendary for its customer service, knows the value of investing in employees. Its chairman, Robert Wegman, attributes the company's reputation for quality service to investment in its workforce.

"No matter what we have invested in our people, we've gotten more in return. I have always believed that our path to great customer service began with that investment."

Employees are your most important assets, and everyone on your payroll should be contributing to your company's success. As a leader, it's your job to make that happen.

Epilogue

If you want bigger payoffs from your staff, invest in them.

74

Ask Offenders for Self-Evaluation

Let difficult employees provide an assessment of themselves. This advice may strike you as the equivalent of handing an enemy a platform. But workers tend to be more critical of themselves than their supervisors, according to some attorneys who advocate employee participation in the evaluation process.

Assignment

Convene a small group to look at your evaluation process to make sure it delivers the right kind of information.

Admitting to a problem, especially on paper, is half the battle of solving it.

Extend the employees' participation to evaluations of their supervisors, especially difficult managers. That could provide eye-opening feedback because a wide gap often exists between how managers view themselves and how their subordinates see them. In a survey by Hudson, a New York City staffing company, nearly all managers (92 percent) rated themselves as good managers. But just 67 percent of workers gave their managers favorable reviews. Your evaluation process moves closer to a true portrait of all your employees when you get a look at them from the equivalent of a wide-angle lens.

75

Celebrate Transformations

One of the most impressive awards my local school district hands out at the end of the year is for the most improved student. The award acknowledges those students who went from a rocky start to a smooth finish. Judging from the winners' broad smiles, the recognition of their successful efforts touches them deeply.

It's equally important to acknowledge improved performances in the workplace. When employees who got off to a rocky start revamp their people skills or work habits, acknowledge that progress. Stop by their desk and congratulate them for great teamwork or a solo presentation at a company seminar.

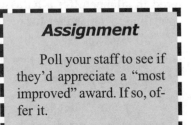

Assignment

Poll your staff to see if they'd appreciate a "most improved" award. If so, offer it.

Consider taking your most-improved employees to lunch. You'll have something positive to talk about for a change.

Also take the time to acknowledge your own efforts. You helped bring about the transformation, after all. The proud feelings will remind you that you win when you bring out the best in your staff.

76

Warding Off Harassers

A coworker confided that she was weary of a male coworker's repeated invitations to visit his apartment. The woman, who is married, had never expressed interest in visiting him and was offended by his requests. I suggested she tell him she had to see when her husband was available. That lifted her spirits.

When a colleague makes inappropriate remarks, go on the offensive and respond with something he doesn't want to hear, especially something involving a husband or a boyfriend. I've heard far too many stories of women who suffered in silence after a harasser struck. You may wind up appealing to a manager for help. But until you do, when the harasser throws something unexpected your way, throw something unexpected right back.

> **Assignment**
>
> Ask your company to bring in an expert to talk about the laws regarding sexual harassment.

Remind the harassers that their behavior is illegal and could cost them their jobs. Ask them if they'd like you to e-mail them more information on that. Of course, if the harassing progresses to inappropriate touching, report that behavior immediately to a supervisor. Short of that, take a stand and let the harasser know you're no easy mark.

> **Epilogue**
> Put sexual harassers on the defensive by telling them what they don't want to hear.

77

Discourage Racist Jokes

Humor is more than a good laugh. It's a facilitator in the office. Humor defuses tension, lifts morale, and builds bonds. Those positive elements affect how you view your job.

Research has shown that "widespread positive humor," increases job satisfaction by 5 percent, writes author David Niven in *The 100 Simple Secrets of Successful People*.

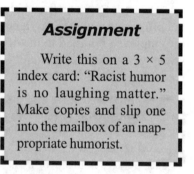

Assignment

Write this on a 3 × 5 index card: "Racist humor is no laughing matter." Make copies and slip one into the mailbox of an inappropriate humorist.

By contrast, 41 percent of employees consider negative humor as a "source of division in their office."

Those are good business reasons to avoid telling or listening to jokes that go for laughs at the expense of women, minorities, immigrants, or the disabled. When a coworker tells such a joke in your presence, tell him or her it's inappropriate. If the racists have no audience, they will have little reason to traffic in such offensive material.

> ## Epilogue
> *Appropriate humor contributes to the well-being of an office.*

78

Asking a Collegue to Clean Up His Cube

The colleague of a friend literally aired his dirty laundry in the office one day. After a rigorous workout at a nearby gym, the employee returned to the office and decided to air dry his sweaty gym clothes by draping them over his cubicle walls. The odor prompted such an outcry that his supervisor ordered the man to return the clothes to his gym bag.

Some employees blur the lines between home and cube. And you may occasionally have to remind them of that difference and the need to tidy up their little space. A colleague who worked with a lot of files

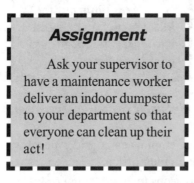

Assignment

Ask your supervisor to have a maintenance worker deliver an indoor dumpster to your department so that everyone can clean up their act!

spread them around his cubicle. The excess spilled into the aisle. People had to step over the documents constantly during the day. Someone finally complained and he condensed the errant filing system. Another colleague stacked books in teetering piles that seemed to come crashing down only on his day off. Someone else had to clean up the mess.

When you ask clutterers to clean up they may wonder what all the fuss is about and become defensive. So tread lightly. Explain how the untidiness affects you and give examples. Soften your approach by offering to help with the clean up. Don't ask a friend how she can live with such clutter. Instead, make some gentle suggestions about where she could store some items.

"Act as if you're giving friendly advice," says Stephen M. Pollan, author of *Lifescripts: What to say to get what you want in life's toughest situations.*

"Avoid coming across as superior. Don't put her down."

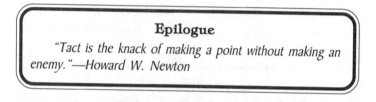

Epilogue

"Tact is the knack of making a point without making an enemy."—Howard W. Newton

79

Don't Take Disputes Personally

A dictionary definition of a cubical office could read: "A fragile ecosystem prone to instant flare-ups." The closeness produces an environment that crackles with tension from repeated interruptions, shouting, and other discourtesies. It's not surprising that a Cornell University study concluded that "open-office environments, especially cubicles, reduce individual performances and productivity."

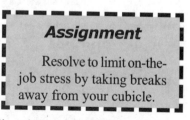

Assignment

Resolve to limit on-the-job stress by taking breaks away from your cubicle.

The key to handling conflict in this compressed environment is to give yourself a wide berth mentally. Start by remembering that a compact environment exaggerates disputes. If a colleague has a difficult personality to begin with, her reactions will probably be even more dramatic in the sardine-like environment of a cube farm.

If a colleague who is given to high drama lashes into you, tell yourself not to take it personally. So often in a tense environment an attack far outweighs the offense. If you did indeed commit a slight that prompted the tirade, acknowledge it, apologize, and move on. If the colleague ratchets up the hostility, disarm her with: "What do you need me to do?" That puts the onus on her and keeps you focused on a solution. Most importantly it takes a positive approach to a very negative situation.

Epilogue

Difficult colleagues become even more so in a cubicle setting. Don't take their outbursts personally.

80

Talking to a Colleague About Faulty Hygiene

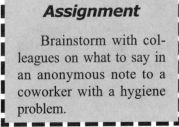

Assignment

Brainstorm with colleagues on what to say in an anonymous note to a coworker with a hygiene problem.

The American Society for Microbiology found that as many as 1/3 of the people who used the restrooms in the country's major airports didn't wash their hands afterwards. That's a lot of people with some odd notions about personal hygiene.

Faulty hygiene, as many of us know all too well, is also a workplace problem. Few people can work up the nerve, though, to tell someone they smell bad or shouldn't pick through the tray of cookies with their hands. But when you work in close proximity with someone with a hygiene problem you must do something to get the person to correct it. Otherwise the distraction will affect your work.

Try the secret-friend approach to avoid embarrassing the person. Send the person an anonymous note that says, "Your body odor belies what a sweet person you are. This is a note from someone who cares." Your compassion and anonymity will probably work wonders.

Epilogue

You owe it to yourself and others to tell a colleague to clean up her act.

81

Try Role-Playing Before the Big Face-Off

Role-playing isn't just for actors. Before a face-to-face conversation with a difficult colleague, try a little role-playing yourself. Stand before a mirror or sit in a chair and imagine you are confronting your workplace foe.

The role-playing accomplishes so much. For one thing, you're not rehearsing and performing at the same time during your big discussion. You will be

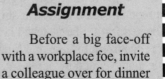

Assignment

Before a big face-off with a workplace foe, invite a colleague over for dinner and role-playing.

calmer and better focused as a result. For another, role-playing is a trial run that will allow you to spot problems in your presentation while you still have the time to correct them and build your confidence.

Take the role-playing a step further and ask a friend or relative to stand in for the colleague and play devil's advocate. That strategy will help you to anticipate objections from your colleague and prepare answers.

Your objective with role-playing shouldn't be to try to control your colleague's behavior. It's clear you can't do that. Rather, the goal should be to keep the troublesome colleague from ruining a performance—yours—that has so much riding on it.

Epilogue

"Confidence and courage come through preparation and practice."—Anonymous

---

82

Getting Colleagues to Respect Your Time

One of the most ambitious people I've ever met was a single parent with three children. After she cleared the dinner table and helped her children with their homework, she did her own homework—studying for a law degree. Time was her most precious commodity back then. It was severely limited and a lot of things competed for it. She watched her time so zealously that she seldom socialized. In time, the time management paid off. She became a lawyer and then a judge.

You may view time as a finite commodity. But some of your colleagues may not. Dawdling is okay with them, because as they see it, they'll always have lots of time to catch up. These colleagues

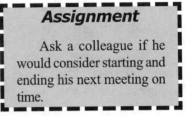

Assignment

Ask a colleague if he would consider starting and ending his next meeting on time.

are the time bandits you'll have to guard against. Otherwise, they will rob you.

They will hold meetings that start late and run over. They're people who share stories that rival the length of ancient sagas. If you're not vigilant, colleagues with their constant instant messages will chip away at a block of time you set aside for research.

You'll have to assume the role of an assertive timekeeper. Show up on time for the meeting and excuse yourself when the agenda veers off course or runs late. Inform the long-winded storytellers that you can hear the rest of their story later. Tell the winged messenger to save her missives until after deadline.

With that approach, you will focus your time on what really matters in the office: work.

Epilogue

Show by your actions that you view time as a precious commodity you have no intentions of squandering.

83

Don't Throw Gas on the Fire

In math, if you add a negative to a negative, you get a bigger negative. On the other hand, if you add a positive to that negative, the negative will decrease or disappear all together.

Assignment

Use this quote for inspiration and motivation: "Getting even with somebody is no way to get ahead of anybody."—Cullen Hightower

That's a good principle to bear in mind when the office hothead confronts you. Knowing how to match his negativity with a positive will move any unpleasant encounter with him toward more positive territory.

One way to do that is to use the element of surprise. Don't match his insults with some of your own. Instead, respond with calmness. Indeed, such an approach is difficult. It calls for a lot more maturity than most people can muster in a confrontation. But it's a strategy that will put you in good company.

In his book *The 7 Habits of Highly Effective People*, author Stephen Covey emphasizes the Win-Win approach, or the art of turning a negative situation into a win for everybody. The ability to do so is a hallmark of emotional maturity.

"If I have it, I can listen, I can emphatically understand, but I can also courageously confront," he says.

Once you master the art of turning down the heat on fiery encounters you can handle any difficult encounters at work with confidence and ease.

Epilogue

Grab some calmness and use it as the fire extinguisher for office hotheads.

84

Don't Let the P.D.s Get You Down

Every office has its prima donnas, the creations of their own imagination and of indulgent managers. The P.D.s have an easy rapport with the boss. Their families may even socialize. They receive the best assignments and the best resources to carry out those assignments. Under those circumstances many other employees could produce

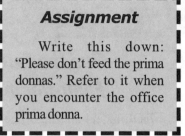

Assignment

Write this down: "Please don't feed the prima donnas." Refer to it when you encounter the office prima donna.

fine work but the prima donnas would never acknowledge that fact.

I once wrote a story about a charity group that distributed used business clothes to low-income women reentering the workplace. The story included a number to call for donations. A prima donna in our office called me to say she had wonderful clothes to donate but was too busy to make the call and drop off the clothes. She wanted me to make the arrangements. I pointed out that I was busy, too. She ended the conversation in a huff and was cool toward me from that day on. Prima donnas thrive on being indulged. They have no compunction about imposing on others, but they feel put upon when others do the same. For your own sake and the sake of the office, please don't feed the prima donnas.

Epilogue
Office prima donnas consider themselves above you. But you should consider that kind of thinking beneath you.

85

Find the Fault Line of the Fault-finding Teammate

Faultfinders are the office con artists. They try to prove their intellectual superiority by finding fault with others. Yet they usually have no alternatives to offer. Instead well-timed and well-aimed criticism is their currency.

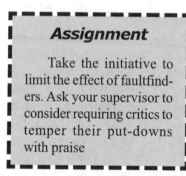

Assignment

Take the initiative to limit the effect of faultfinders. Ask your supervisor to consider requiring critics to temper their put-downs with praise

Faultfinders think nothing of discounting a colleague's hard work by seizing on tiny flaws in her presentation. Valerie Pierce, the author of *Quick Thinking on Your Feet: The art of thriving under pressure*, calls such speaker abuse, "a very lazy way of winning the argument, since we don't have to bother with the content of the discussion."

Yet the strategy packs a punch, Pierce says. "This is very powerful as it diverts the attention of the victim. When you are on the receiving end of this, it can be totally debilitating."

Fortunately the faultfinders can be easily disarmed. And one question usually does the trick: "Can you suggest any alternatives?" That puts the spotlight on the critic, where it should be. When that happens the critic usually has very little to say.

Epilogue

"Any fool can criticize, condemn, and complain—and most fools do."—Dale Carnegie

Know Your Workplace Rights

A few years ago the U.S. Equal Employment Opportunity Commission began an outreach program aimed at educating teen workers about their right to work free of sexual harassment and other abuses. One of the agency's biggest surprises after meeting with youth groups was to learn that teens didn't know what actions constituted sexual harassment. Many of them had endured uncomfortable behavior on the job without knowing they had experienced sexual harassment.

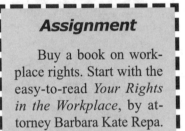

Assignment

Buy a book on workplace rights. Start with the easy-to-read *Your Rights in the Workplace*, by attorney Barbara Kate Repa.

Knowledge truly is power when it comes to your workplace rights. Knowing your rights means that you know that your company has to ensure that its workplace is safe and free of discrimination and harassment.

You don't have to put up with illegal behavior. When colleagues send you inappropriate messages, send them an e-mail apprising them of your rights and their potential liability to the company. The more you know about your rights, the better you can state your case. You have no reason to suffer abuse in silence or in ignorance.

Epilogue

Help safeguard your workplace rights by learning what they are.

87

Confront Bullies on Your Own Terms

I once handed a colleague some information about a photograph that was going to run with a story I wrote. She's a person known for her temper. And people tread lightly around her. She glanced at the information and shoved it back into my hand.

"This is incomplete!" she yelled, loud enough to catch the attention of people nearby.

I looked her in the eye and calmly said, "I'm sorry some information is missing. I will get it. But I don't appreciate being talked to like that."

> ### Assignment
>
> In a run-in with a bully, stay focused on what you need.
>
> The strategy will help you remain calm so you can muster an effective response.

She apologized. I got the rest of the information. And the dispute ended. I could have easily shoved the paper back at her, to spark the equivalent of a verbal smack down, but I didn't take the bait. If I had, I wouldn't have accomplished my goal of taking care of a bully on my own terms.

Epilogue
"Pugnacity is a form of courage, but a very bad form."
—Sinclair Lewis

Establish Rules for Contentious Team Meetings

Teamwork can be an exhilarating experience. The rush of ideas and the possibility of solving a problem or creating a new product is heady stuff. A fully functioning team is a real powerhouse.

"When working effectively, a team can make better decisions, solve more complex problems and do more to enhance creativity and build skills than individuals working alone," writes management expert Ken Blanchard in *Leading at a Higher Level: Blanchard on leadership and creating high performing organizations.*

But a team can also be a font of utter frustration. When underperforming teammates fail to meet deadlines or produce work that is decidedly under-

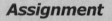

> ### *Assignment*
>
> After a deadline, list the plusses and minuses of your current team to determine what changes you need to make.

whelming they nullify the advantages of working as a unit. You as a team leader may be forced to take corrective action as a deadline looms and the stakes are high and the pressure is on. Team meetings during this time could be downright ugly.

"Deadline might bring out the worst," said Joanne, the Pittsburgh consultant. Rather than focus on teammates' negatives when procedures break down at the 11th hour, focus on the members' strengths. You will energize them.

"It's always better that people feel empowered and that we are working with them to determine how we meet the goal," Sujansky says. The difficult conversations on performance should wait until deadline passes.

> **Epilogue**
> *When restoring unity to a team, decide what it needs and when it needs it.*

89

Outing the Backstabber

Backstabbers are the office termites. They cause a great deal of damage behind the scenes. They live to make a name for themselves at the expense of others. Their modus operandi is to talk themselves up to the boss while badmouthing others. They speak first and check their facts later, if ever. The way to put a stop to their hurtful ways is to challenge them. They can seldom withstand the openness.

> **Assignment**
>
> Use this for inspiration: "The greatest homage we can pay to truth is to use it."
> —Ralph Waldo Emerson

A colleague known for spreading unkind gossip once announced to a group of coworkers, including Sherry, that the company cafeteria owner was mean to his wife. Some in the group grumbled that maybe they should think twice about patronizing the place. Sherry asked the gossiper what he based his conclusion on since the man spoke to his wife in Arabic. The language has some full, explosive sounds that could leave the impression that people are arguing even when they aren't. He had no response to that.

Backstabbers seldom survive head-on confrontations. That's why they're called backstabbers. If you don't challenge them, eventually you will have a bull's eye on your back.

Epilogue

The best way to control the backstabber is to smoke him out with the truth.

90
When a Colleague Refuses to Cooperate

Seated at her desk, Kayla was speaking to a client by phone but was unable to hear. Kayla's cubical neighbors, who were having a lively discussion, drowned her client's voice out. She wanted to ask them to lower their voices, but she hesitated. One of the women was known for her temper. Finally, though, Kayla grew tired of asking her client to repeat himself. So she turned to the women and politely asked them to keep the noise down. The short-fused coworker snapped back, "Well you didn't lower your voice when I was talking on the phone the other day."

Kayla, determined to keep things civil and get back to the client, said firmly, "You should have said something. I apologize for that. But for now I need you to lower your voice." The woman complied.

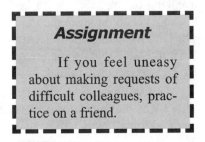

Assignment

If you feel uneasy about making requests of difficult colleagues, practice on a friend.

Situations like that never resolve themselves properly unless you stand your ground. No colleague should interfere with your work and when you challenge their disruptive behavior the right thing for the person to do is to refrain immediately. But combative, stubborn colleagues will resent requests and refuse to comply. Kayla's coworker wanted to pull her into a game of tit for tat, when all Kayla needed was a quieter room.

When you meet such resistance, calmly, directly, and firmly restate what you need. That is about the only way to knock a stubborn colleague off their very wobbly soapbox.

Epilogue
"Stubbornness is the strength of the weak."
—*Swiss theologian John Kaspar Lavater*

91

Challenge the Chronic Complainer

The chronic complainers are the conspiracy theorists of the office. They see negativity everywhere. While employees generally have plenty to gripe about, the chronic complainers carry the grousing to an extreme. In their eyes, they are the only people who do good work or show commitment or integrity. They constantly look for confirmation of those beliefs and they discount any facts that challenge their philosophy on life.

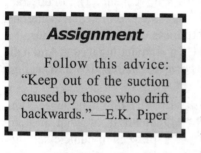

Assignment

Follow this advice: "Keep out of the suction caused by those who drift backwards."—E.K. Piper

I parted ways with a long-time friend at work because of her toxic ways. She savaged so many people behind their backs, including some people for whom I have the highest respect. I challenged her notion of universal incompetence at work by pointing out some good work someone had done. She minimized the person's efforts. She wasn't interested in building people up. Her goal was to tear them down.

After a while the constant complaining began to feel like a weight and I found it unbearable to be around her. Plus, I didn't want to be deemed guilty of being a grouser by association. So I ended the friendship. Sometimes the best way to manage a toxic relationship is to abandon it.

> **Epilogue**
> *Choose as friends those colleagues who share your values.*

92

The Cell Phone and What Ails Us

A woman who uses her cell phone exclusively at home accidentally left it at work over a weekend. The phone rang frequently with a tinny rock tune. She didn't call in to alert her colleagues about her forgetfulness or to ask them to turn the phone off. She just resigned herself to letting it ring. And it did frequently until a frustrated coworker marched over to her desk and turned it off.

> **Assignment**
>
> Ask your supervisor if you could draw up a list of cell-phone etiquette do's and don't's and distribute it to the staff.

Cell-phone abuse is emblematic of what ails employees in cubicle settings. Etiquette has yet to catch up to the setting.

"All cubicles do is fuel rage—especially if the transformation to cubicles is not accompanied by civility training," says Giovinella Gonthier in *Rude Awakenings: Overcoming the Civility Crisis in the Workplace.*

Cell-phone abuse is one of the most visible manifestations of cubicle discourtesies. The breaches range from people talking too loud, to choosing intrusive ring-tones, or to leaving the phones on and unattended. I love Beethoven's *Ode to Joy* and his *Fifth Symphony*. But I detest them both as dreary ring tones.

If a colleague's cell phone is causing ringing in your ears, politely ask him to turn the volume down. And if he frequently leaves behind a cell phone when he goes to lunch, leaving you and others to suffer, ask the person to turn it off or take it with him. If the person forgets the cell phone after your talk, ask his permission to go over and turn the phone off.

Epilogue

Cell phone abuse adds to the deterioration of cubical life.

93

Keeping Delicate Phone Talks Private

I once worked next to a guy with a host of medical problems. He frequently conferred with his doctors. One day he hit a medical trifecta. He spoke with his cardiologist, proctologist, and internist. Because the man didn't moderate his voice I caught an awful case of TMI—Too Much Information.

He talked about very private matters as if he were discussing the weather. And the indiscretions overwhelmed me. At times I simply had to walk away. Or I would use the time during his consultations to go for

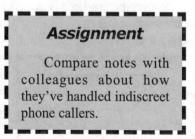

Assignment

Compare notes with colleagues about how they've handled indiscreet phone callers.

coffee or stop by a friend's cubicle. At other times I put on earplugs and cranked up the music. While those methods succeeded in drowning him out, they didn't go to the heart of the problem, which I faced over and over again. His conversations were much too intimate for public consumption.

I finally worked up my nerve to take a more direct approach, which really is the best strategy when you're dealing with a conflict. After he finished one of his calls I said,

"I really enjoyed that three-way call with your doctor. I hope you mend really soon." I seldom had a problem with him again.

If you want colleagues to show discretion, you may have to help them along.

Epilogue

At work, discretion far too often gets the boot.

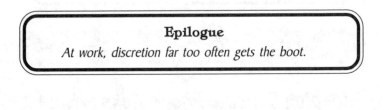

Imagine Success

People who practice visualization swear by its power to make their wishes come true. Those who practice focus intently on a mental image of what they want to manifest in their life. They believe that if they focus on what they want, it will materialize. At its core visualization is like positive thinking with a little Zen added.

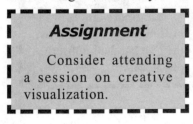

Assignment

Consider attending a session on creative visualization.

120

Positive thinking is a powerful force.

"Whether you think can or can't, you're right," said Henry Ford.

Determine what you'd like to achieve. Perhaps you'd like to react more calmly to your foe's outburst or you'd like to be more assertive.

Take a few minutes each day to reflect on what you want to achieve. Hold the thought in your mind as you focus on your breath. Keep going until you feel relaxed. Keep your image in your mind the whole time.

When your spirits are low because of constant battles with a problem coworker try to imagine success. You've got nothing to lose by devoting time and energy to something you want.

Epilogue
Every great project begins with a healthy dose of wishful thinking.

95

How to Handle a Surprise Milestone Party

In an ageist society such as ours, some employees go to great lengths to play down their age. Even increasing numbers of men are dyeing their hair and turning to plastic surgery to look younger than their years.

So the last thing people like that want is for someone to call attention to their age through a milestone party at work. The organizers of such events, usually much younger colleagues, believe

Assignment

Poll your older colleagues on milestone parties. If they dislike them, have them send an e-mail to the office organizer asking her to nix the milestone parties.

the fetes are a fun way to mark important birthdays. Boy, are they off the mark.

I know of workers who have taken the day off to avoid being singled out for being of a certain age. Or they pressure the organizers to call off the festivities.

If you are dreading the day because you can't take it off, relax and take command of the ceremony. Draw up a list of reasons why getting older is better, sort of like David Letterman's Top-Ten Lists. When you are asked to speak, read the list and make every word count.

For example, you might say, "Now that I'm 55, my IQ trumps that of the person giving this party."

If you take control of the party, you can show up the idea for what it is: a very bad one.

Epilogue

Even if you have to face a milestone birthday party, it's still your party. Seize, don't cede, control.

96

Oh Lunch Most Foul!

I teach an etiquette class to elementary school children at my local library. I tell them it's bad manners to talk with a mouth full of food or to blow their noses at the table. When I eat lunch with coworkers I often think I should raise the maximum age for the class.

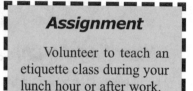

Assignment

Volunteer to teach an etiquette class during your lunch hour or after work.

Some adults simply have strange table manners. While at lunch with five coworkers in the company cafeteria, four of them blew their noses during the meal without turning away or without even saying "Excuse me." Blowing one's nose at the table tops most etiquette lists as the most disgusting thing people do during a meal.

My experience certainly made my stomach queasy. I came close to swearing off lunch with any of my nose-blowing colleagues. But I found them interesting. And lunch is a great time to get to know colleagues better and learn about company lore.

While at lunch with one of the offenders who had just cleared his nose, I pointed out that he made it hard for me to face my yogurt. He apologized. And the next time at lunch, he stepped away to blow his nose. I was on my way to an appetizing lunch hour again.

It's uncomfortable to point out colleagues' shortcomings, but if the price of not pointing them out is too steep, you owe it to yourself to speak up.

Epilogue

When disturbingly bad manners come between you and a likable colleague, work on their manners.

97

Handling the Chronic Interrupter

The chronic interrupter is the office narcissist. They believe their needs are the most important and they want them met instantly, and they will insist that the world do just that.

A coworker once insisted on sharing some family vacation pictures with me while I was on deadline. I told her I would look at them later. After an hour, while I was still hard at work, she asked again if I wanted to look at the pictures. Once more I said I would look later.

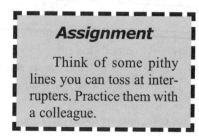

Assignment

Think of some pithy lines you can toss at interrupters. Practice them with a colleague.

After the third request I had to give a more dead-on answer: "As I've said, I am busy now. When I am ready to look at them I will let you know."

That stopped her insistence. As promised, when I finished my work, I looked at her pictures.

It would have been easy for me to refuse to look at the pictures because the woman was so annoying. But it was important for me to keep my word. And I really wanted to share in her joy over the pictures.

With chronic interrupters you have to set boundaries because they are unable to. In meetings or in casual conversations you'll have to ask them to stop interrupting you, and in the heat of deadline you'll have to demand that they hold off on their requests.

If you don't set boundaries their intrusive behavior will drive the relationship. And emotionally they are much too young to be at the wheel.

> **Epilogue**
> *Set boundaries to keep the chronic interrupters at bay.*

Don't Let an Aggressive Colleague Commandeer Your Meeting

I've seen it happen so often. A colleague chairs a meeting and curmudgeonly coworkers set out to undermine her authority. The curmudgeons particularly like to challenge a coworker's authority when a manager is present. Nothing could make the meeting-wreckers happier than to engineer your meltdown with the boss as a witness. The wreckers generally succeed with people who are unprepared and unsure of themselves. They fail when the person running the meeting makes it clear by her assertiveness and efficiency that she is in charge. If you master just a few mechanics you can keep the meeting-wreckers at bay. First remind yourself that you have the authority to run the meeting. Everything stems from that: the topics of discussion, the recognition of speakers, the time limits on speaking. If an overbear-

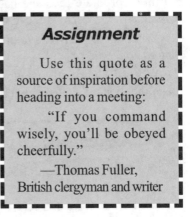

Assignment

Use this quote as a source of inspiration before heading into a meeting:

"If you command wisely, you'll be obeyed cheerfully."

—Thomas Fuller, British clergyman and writer

ing colleague rattles on, ask him or her to wrap up so other views can be heard. If the person speaks out of turn, ask the person to wait. When meeting-wreckers succeed they make you act defensively. Then you lose credibility and authority. By mastering a few mechanics you can retain control of a meeting.

Epilogue

To paraphrase a Biblical observation, "No meeting can serve two masters."

Mind the Generational Gap

Working with several generations of colleagues can be an enriching experience, but prejudices and arrogance can turn that asset into the liability of generational warfare. I once told a younger colleague that I was excited about participating in a 3.5-mile corporate race she had always run in. She quickly responded, "Oh yeah, you can walk it.

I shot back, "I also have the option of running it, which I plan to do."

When dealing with a colleague of a different generation make the most of the encounters.

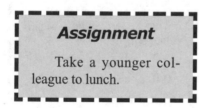

Assignment

Take a younger colleague to lunch.

To do that check your prejudices. Many Boomers, the first generation to wholeheartedly embrace workouts, are still running in their 40s and 50s and 60s.

If you're older, bridge the gap by sharing some of your most memorable experiences from your years with the company.

Many younger workers appreciate office lore and take great pride in an office with a rich history. Sharing your stories will feed their hunger for company culture and build bonds at the same time.

If you're a younger worker, offer your help when an older worker has a tech problem at work you can solve. As an older more experienced worker, you may possess a wealth of knowledge about your field. Share that knowledge when colleagues ask. A younger colleague considers me the office grammarian. When she asks, I cheerfully share my expertise with her.

By no means should you patronize someone older or younger. And don't pretend to be a know-it-all because of your years or over self-confidence. By minding the generational gap you build bridges, rather than burning them.

Epilogue

"A great many people think they are thinking when they are merely rearranging their prejudices." —Philosopher William James

---

100

Discourage Eavesdropping

In the realm of office gossips, eavesdroppers are some of the most determined and most crafty. They gather information through stealthy means to put their coworkers in the worst light. They will use it to get a leg up on a rival for a promotion. They plant the seeds of doubt about the person's abilities. As British philosopher and mathematician Bertrand Russell said, "No one gossips about other people's secret virtues."

Assignment

Challenge an eaves-dropper to say something good about his targets.

The eavesdroppers' modus operandi is to position themselves near a conversation and tune in as if they are on a reconnaissance mission. In a way they are. Be careful not to help the eavesdropper along. Beware of other people around you when you are discussing sensitive matters with another colleague. If you have to make a call regarding sensitive personal matters, moderate your voice. If an eavesdropper with keen hearing picks up on something in your conversation and later quizzes you about it, tell them that the matter was private and that you hope he or she will respect it as such.

The best way to handle eavesdroppers is to make sure they don't hear any private information about you in the first place. So, if you reside in a cubicle, borrow a manager's office for sensitive phone calls. If that isn't possible, make the call before office hours or afterward, when few to no people are around.

Epilogue

Don't unwittingly make yourself easy prey for eavesdroppers.

101
Extending a Helping Hand

"You cannot contribute to something significant without being changed," writes management expert John Maxwell in *The 360° Leader: Developing your influence from anywhere in the organization.* If you want to be better than you are, become part of something bigger than you are."

That "something bigger" could be mentoring a floundering colleague. Both you and your company will benefit from your generosity. One of the casualties of today's lean and mean office

is the extra time needed for staff development. Managers are so squeezed that they have to take the sink or swim approach with new employees. As an experienced employee, you could fill in the gap.

How do you know if a colleague is worth mentoring? Some experts say you should gauge whether an employee is "teachable." The teachable employee isn't afraid to admit her deficiencies and will ask what she needs to improve.

You can help her achieve what might otherwise be impossible without the help of a mentor.

Epilogue

Successful mentoring is a win-win strategy for you and your company.

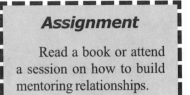

Taming the Green-Eyed Monster

Less than two hours into his new job as CEO of pharmaceutical giant Pfizer Inc., Jeffrey B. Kindler began mending fences. He reached out to two rivals who lost out to him, according to the *Wall Street Journal*.

"I need your help. The company needs your help," Kindler told them.

> **Assignment**
>
> Send a thank-you note to a colleague who lost out to you in a promotion.
>
> Tell the person you look forward to having him on your team.

Even at exalted levels, executives have to work to tame the green-eyed monster. People further down the ranks have to do the same. If you beat out a colleague for a promotion, you have some fence-mending to do too, especially if you continue to work closely with that co-worker. Convert venom into honey by frequently asking the employee's advice, and by thanking him for giving it. Take the colleague to lunch, and remind the person how important his contributions are to the company.

You may not be able to prevent jealous feelings, but you can help transform them into emotions that are helpful to you and your colleagues.

Epilogue
A tamed green-eyed monster is less likely to bite.

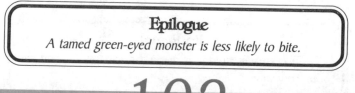

103

Makes Sure the Boss Knows Your Side of the Story

An administrative assistant who worked for Vernice, the marketing firm owner in Kansas City, Missouri, was the office tattle-tale and frequently used that role to wield power when the boss was away.

"You just wait until Vernice hears about this," she often intoned.

And as soon as Vernice returned, the woman rushed in with a laundry list of her colleagues so-called transgressions. The woman was trying to score points at her colleagues' expense.

If your office arch nemesis is such a person, make sure you drop in on the boss occasionally to determine

Assignment

"Truth abhors a vacuum." Write this time-honored advice on a post-it note and stick on your computer as a reminder to make sure boss hears your side of the story.

what he or she has been hearing. A good manager will discount tattle-tellers, but others may take them seriously.

When you get an audience with the boss, don't tattletale to get back at your colleague. Frame your visit as a time to give the boss updates on a team project you're working on, for example. Mention the disagreements with your colleague. And tell how you have resolved them. That should show the boss who is the more trustworthy bearer of news.

Epilogue

A tattle-teller is your office blind spot. Widen your field of vision by making sure the boss knows your side of the story.

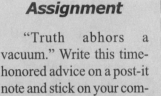

Recovering From a Fall

Cindy, an administrative assistant, suffered constant stress because of a nagging coworker. The hypercritical colleague was a perfectionist who constantly complained about Cindy.

The last straw broke when the woman complained about having to cover the phones after Cindy left for an afternoon doctor's appointment.

When Cindy returned two hours later, the woman asked Cindy about what she considered a long absence. Feeling overwhelmed. Cindy burst and spewed obscenities at the woman. Other coworkers looked on in disbelief. Her foe remained calm. Cindy was the one the boss reprimanded. Not her foe.

Rightly or wrongly, you have to do damage control after a foe causes you to lose it. Don't justify the meltdown. Instead, apologize to the boss for the disruption. Voice your regrets to colleagues over lunch. Keep the remarks short. Just admit that the display of anger was inappropriate and you're sorry for the disruption. When you are sincere, people will forgive and forget. After all, they're probably familiar with your foe's antics. They know they might have reacted the same way

---

Epilogue

"The greatest accomplishment is not in never falling, but in rising again after you fall."—Confucius

---

105
Empower Yourself

The person who can most assure your success in dealing with difficult people is you. Sure, you may, on occasion, need to turn to colleagues or a supervisor for help. But for the most part you'll have to face down troublesome colleagues all by yourself. If you have any weak points in your defense system, shore up.

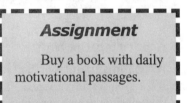

Assignment

Buy a book with daily motivational passages.

For example, if you've spent your life avoiding conflict or if you cave when an overbearing colleague disagrees with you, you may suffer from low self-esteem. For people with a poor self-image, any conflict, especially one in the office, produces an overwhelming sense of helplessness. Build a sense of empowerment by first acknowledging low self-esteem. Then figure out how to lift it. Finding a helpful book on the topic is a good start. One of my favorites is *Self-Esteem: A proven program of cognitive techniques for assessing, improving and maintaining your self-esteem* by Matthew McKay and Patrick Fanning. If your problems are deeply entrenched you may need therapy to overcome low self-esteem. Your company's benefits may cover most, if not all, of the costs of counseling sessions through an Employee Assistance Program. The dividends you'll gain from investing in your emotional well-being will be enormous. You'll find that when you operate from a strong foundation, the office troublemakers can't unnerve you.

Epilogue

"Nothing can stop the man with the right mental attitude from achieving his goal; nothing on earth can help the man with the wrong mental attitude."—Thomas Jefferson

106

Seek a Colleague's Advice

A longtime friend who had just received her PH.D. called me in tears. She was convinced her former adviser, with whom she frequently clashed, was hamstringing her efforts to land a university teaching job. She said she had applied to 70 universities. Some seemed interested in her, she said, until they conferred with her old school. She had given up.

> ### Assignment
>
> Draw some imaginary ice cream scoops on a piece of paper. Label them with your options for dealing with an office foe. Ask friends for suggestions. Draw scoops for their ideas. On a clean sheet of paper build an ice-cream cone with the best ideas.

I reminded her that the country has about 2,600 accredited, four-year colleges and universities. She had only contacted a fraction. With so many other schools out there, she was declaring defeat prematurely. Before she sent out another application, I suggested that she have a candid sit-down with her adviser to see if they couldn't reach a truce and hammer out a new response when prospective employers called. My friend took comfort in that.

Before you declare defeat with a difficult colleague, seek the advice of a trusted colleague. Another pair of eyes might see opportunity where you only see defeat.

Epilogue
More eyes and ears, more opportunities.

107

Ask for Backup

Kelly, a young newcomer to her office, felt uncomfortable with overtures from a much older male coworker. He frequently invited her to lunch in the cafeteria and offered to give her rides home. He would sometimes pull up a chair near her cubicle to talk. Unsure of how to voice her discomfort to him, she confided in an older female coworker who sat nearby. That woman talked to the man and told him to back off. He protested but eventually left the woman alone.

Sometimes speaking up against inappropriate

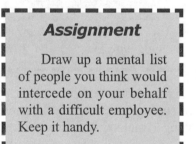

Assignment

Draw up a mental list of people you think would intercede on your behalf with a difficult employee. Keep it handy.

behavior is unbearably difficult. If you're new on the job, young, or are simply determined to make a good first impression, you're less inclined to stand up to a bully, backstabber, or harasser. But your more experienced coworkers may feel perfectly comfortable speaking up on your behalf. Take advantage of that.

Epilogue
The "co" in "coworker" reflects that we're all in this together.

135

108

Temper Criticism With Praise

Bob Miglani grew up serving chili dogs and chocolate-dipped cones at his family's Dairy Queen store in New Jersey. When a customer dropped an ice cream cone, the store replaced it free of charge. No questions. No arguments.

Why the policy, which seemed to benefit the customer much more than the store? "Because it preserves the integrity of our business and it's the right thing to do," he says.

> **Assignment**
>
> Make it easy to praise a nemesis by imagining the move as part of an "Opposite Day."

To preserve the integrity of your relationship with a difficult colleague you may have to perform the unexpected at times. That could well include praising the colleague when the person does something right. It won't be easy. It takes a lot of courage to rise above the natural instinct to belittle everything a troublemaker does.

People skilled at dealing with the public know how important it is to strike a balance. Even under fire from irate customers, those workers can rise above anger and admit when customers are right. The workers simply know how disarming honest praise can be.

> **Epilogue**
> *In interpersonal dealings, the unexpected sometimes is your best weapon.*

109

Reject Offensive E-Mails

The former CEO of Boeing Co. was coaxed out of retirement to lead the company through a turbulent period. But the man, a father and grandfather, was later forced out of the top job after his love affair with another company executive was discovered through a trail of steamy e-mails.

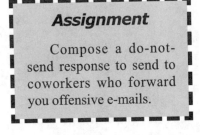

Assignment

Compose a do-not-send response to send to coworkers who forward you offensive e-mails.

Questionable e-mails have sunk many ships in the workplace and will probably sink many more because companies have grown increasingly intolerant of e-mail faux pas. Yet some employees haven't gotten the message and they cheerfully traffic in racist or pornographic e-mails. Some employees believe the materials are harmless and entertaining and eagerly share them. But some companies aren't amused and have fired employees on the spot for offensive e-mails.

Ignore such e-mails or ask a colleague to stop sending them. Trafficking in risky e-mails has become more risky than ever.

Epilogue

The only thing standing between you and unemployment could be an offensive e-mail. Never forward one.

110

Change Your Location if You Have To

When do you need to move your chair? Carla had to consider that question while dealing with a micromanaging team leader. The woman would rewrite Carla's reports and, by many accounts, make them worse. She sometimes took credit for the research, but if she accidentally inserted an error, she blamed Carla. When Carla complained, the woman retaliated by "forgetting" to pass on information about last-minute meetings.

> ### Assignment
>
> Make a list of the pros and cons of continuing to work with a difficult colleague. Add them up. The higher number wins.

Carla's misery didn't end there. She sat next to the woman, who often commented on Carla's conversations with clients. Carla spoke with the woman's manager several times. That stopped the retaliatory behavior for a while but it always resumed. Finally, Carla asked for and was granted a transfer to a new team and a new seat.

She considered herself weak for being unable to rectify her situation, but the bottom line is that if your location prevents you from doing a good job, you have to change your location.

Epilogue

"Put yourself into a different room, that's what the mind is for."—Novelist Margaret Atwood

---

111

Meet the Office Recluse

Kate often commented how a coworker would breeze by her in the hall and say absolutely nothing. When she ventured a greeting, it was returned with a grunt. She finally gave up in anger.

One day though, he came over to her cubicle and greeted her as if he had suddenly discovered her existence. Turns out he needed a telephone number. She supplied the number. The next time they passed in the hall, she was prepared to speak but he had reverted

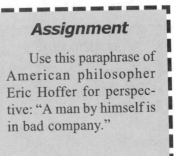

Assignment

Use this paraphrase of American philosopher Eric Hoffer for perspective: "A man by himself is in bad company."

to his usual behavior. Her anger toward him grew. She felt used. But it was a waste of time to take the slight personally, though. The recluse treated everyone the same.

Just imagine a day without sharing a good joke or without a shoulder to lean on. That's the reality of the office recluse. They deserve pity more than anger.

Epilogue

The office recluse prefers a shell, not a well-intentioned coworker with a nutcracker.

112

Pick Your Battles

Sometimes I receive letters that I dub the "Kitchen Sink Chronicles." The list of complaints about a problem coworker spans so many areas that it's hard to know where to begin. The litany reflects employees who are battling on too many fronts.

Troublemakers always give you plenty to complain about. But if you complain about every infraction, you turn into a whiner, another category of problematic employees.

Assignment

Reality Check: For a day list the things you talk about. If complaints reign, resolve to cut back on them.

Choose your battles. Otherwise your constant complaining will drive away the colleagues whose support you need.

If you find your colleagues changing the subject quickly when you talk about your office problems, that's your cue to cut back. Choose well your battles as well as your moments to talk about them.

Epilogue

"A fanatic is one who can't change his mind and won't change the subject."—Sir Winston Churchill

---

140

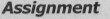

113

Have Grudge, Will Travel

About the only thing worse than being stuck in an office with a coworker who gives you heartburn is being stuck on a business trip with her. If the person is obnoxious in the office she may be absolutely unbearable in the more compressed environment of a car or airplane.

Assignment

Before a dreaded road trip, write down your options for opting out of a conversation with an intrusive colleague.

Braggarts are particularly hard to withstand on the road because of their incessant prattle. Minimize the intrusive conversations by taking a cue from seasoned travelers. Pack a deep supply of distractions: An Ipod, laptop, and books. And tell the talkative coworker you need time to polish a presentation.

Be polite and engage in brief conversation at times to keep from straining the relationship any further. But don't indulge the fellow traveler any more than you would in the office.

Epilogue

Make sure you're well equipped to survive a road trip with an office foe.

114

When to Take Legal Action

Many employees are driven to file lawsuits because their employers minimized or dismissed their complaints about illegal mistreatment, or the employers branded them as troublemakers for fingering a rainmaker.

Even still, before you take your fight to court, make sure you've exhausted all other options. Did you tell your supervisor? If she did nothing, did you move up the ladder?

Even lawyers who represent employees sound cautionary notes about the high cost of such lawsuits in time, money, and privacy. Nothing should stop you from taking action when your workplace rights have been trampled. But consider a lawsuit only after you see no other way to stop illegal behavior.

Assignment

Call a friend to get a second opinion before deciding whether to file a lawsuit.

Epilogue

A lawsuit should be an option of last resort.

115

Restoring Trust

At some point, your longtime adversary may apologize and want to reestablish a friendship. You should accept the apology. But don't confuse an apology with trust. Trust takes time to regrow.

"Trusting others means relying on others' honesty and commitment to keep their promises to you," writes author Cynthia Wall in *The Courage to Trust: A guide to building deep and lasting relationships*.

An apology can't manufacture a new foundation for trust. But time and effort can.

Keep the lines of communication open to rebuild trust.

Until then, keep your guard up and lower it only when you are sure your opponent's efforts are sincere and worthy of your trust.

Assignment

After a foe apologizes for his actions, write down ideas on what efforts would reestablish trust. Use your list as a guide.

Epilogue
Trust is seldom an overnight sensation.

116
Develop Coping Rituals

Famous writers through the centuries established rituals to prime their minds. German poet Friedrich von Schiller kept rotting apples in his desk so he could inhale their bouquet. Edgar Allen Poe wrote best with a cat perched on his shoulder.

"Rituals help us shift gears, make transitions, change our mental states," says Naomi Epel in *The Observation Deck*.

Develop your own rituals to help you through adversarial encounters at work. When a conversation turns tense, pull gently on your pinky finger to remind yourself to remain calm. Stroke your arm or jangle change in your pocket. Mentally recite a favorite passage. This strategy isn't artful dodging. Instead it's passage to a safe harbor that will provide you shelter during a raging storm.

Epilogue

The consistency of a ritual can provide a source of strength in a battle with a coworker.

117

Beware the False Confidant

Beware the false confidant who tries to pry loose information, with "Oh, come on, you can tell me." If someone has to say that, you have no basis for trust.

People who pump you for information have the prime objective of passing it on.

Keep you secrets to yourself until you know you are dealing with a true confidant. They are rare birds indeed. If you share your deepest

Assignment

Inspiration: "None are so fond of secrets as those who do not mean to keep them."—British sportswriter Charles Caleb Colton secrets with an unconfirmed confidant you could wind up seeding the grapevine at the same time. And past affairs or criticism of a manager could come back to entangle you when you are vying for a promotion against an arch nemesis who knows your secrets. In the Information Age, information is power. Be careful not to empower an enemy.

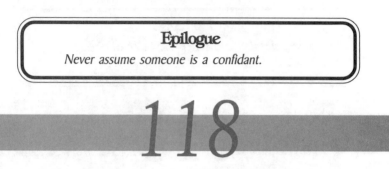

Epilogue

Never assume someone is a confidant.

118

Become a Leader of One

At the center of prolonged personnel conflicts is usually a weak manager who just won't lead. He promises to take on a bully but hates conflict so much he winds up waiting the problem out, instead. David worked for such a boss. He was known as a great listener but a man of inaction. David would complain about an uncoop-

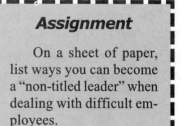

Assignment

On a sheet of paper, list ways you can become a "non-titled leader" when dealing with difficult employees.

erative colleague. The man would nod and promise to investigate. But he did nothing. When you run up against a manager who won't manage conflict, you have to bring in the reserves: yourself. Lead the leader by example. Mark Sanborn, the author of *You Don't Need a Title to Be a Leader*, calls subordinates who take on leadership roles "non-titled leaders."

"The bottom line is, influence and inspiration come from the person, not the position," Sanborn says.

Sometimes you are the best man for the job of fending off a bully. Show the guy luxuriating in the glass office that leadership has to be exercised in order for it to qualify as such.

> **Epilogue**
> Sometimes the best leaders are those who rise to the job naturally.

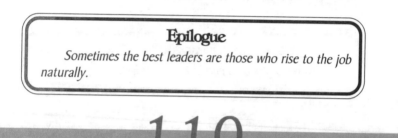

Insist on Respect

Managers set the tone for the office. Their rudeness begets rudeness among employees.

No matter the rank of the impolite person, insist on respect. And you must insist on it even in small ways. If a supervisor breaks into your conversation to speak with a coworker and the coworker turns away from you without an apology, take the lead in setting a different tone. Say to your colleague, "Excuse me. We will pick this up later," or "I see you two need to talk. I will excuse myself." That sends the message that

> **Assignment**
>
> "True life is lived when tiny changes occur."
>
> —Russian author Leo Tolstoy
>
> Refer to this quote to remind yourself of the importance of little social graces.

you want to be treated with respect, no matter the circumstances, or the intruder's rank. Little courtesies don't seem like much to insist on. But they go a long way in building environments where impoliteness finds it hard to thrive.

Epilogue

Take the lead using social graces to counter rude behavior in the office.

120

Become a Peer Mediator

Many high schools have peer mediation programs that train students in the art of settling differences peacefully. Having peers act as mediators makes sense because the students can relate to one another.

You may come naturally to peer mediation in the office. If you do, put your talent to work. Katie did just that after a fierce argument between two colleagues fell just short of fisticuffs.

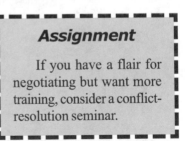

Assignment

If you have a flair for negotiating but want more training, consider a conflict-resolution seminar.

Mike wanted to share a joke he found on the Web with Jason, who sat a few cubicles away. Mike yelled the story out to him. Jason found the joke offensive and called Mike stupid and racist. Mike was mortified. He went over to Jason to apologize. Jason ordered him to go away. He vowed never to speak to him again. Distraught, Mike appealed to Katie. She said she would speak with Jason but told Mike he had to stay away from questionable jokes.

A week or so later, when Jason reiterated his hatred of Mike, Katie saw an opening and sprang into action. She told Jason she understood why he was angry. She thought the joke was inappropriate, too. But she said that Mike has a good heart that is too often obscured by his awkward social graces. She encouraged Jason to accept the apology the next time. He did.

Epilogue

Natural negotiators are the undeputized peace officers of the office.

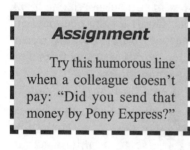

When a Colleague Won't Pay Up

I often hear colleagues gripe about coworkers who borrowed money and never repaid it. The lenders felt awkward asking for the money back; they thought it showed poor manners. So, they resigned themselves to griping about a colleague who didn't pay up. Some people who borrow simply don't assign a high priority to repaying their debts.

Assignment

Try this humorous line when a colleague doesn't pay: "Did you send that money by Pony Express?"

You should establish a lending policy that recovers your debts. Spot colleagues a few dollars for lunch if they ask. If they haven't repaid the money after a few weeks, ask them for the money. Sometimes you may find that the loan just slipped their mind.

Try some humor if necessary to nudge a colleague to pay: "I'm calling in all my debts. Please settle up ASAP, to avoid a hefty interest fee." If the person continuously puts you off, then forget about the debt, resolve never to lend the person money again, and let it go.

Epilogue

"Be careful about lending a friend money. It may damage her memory."—British writer John Ruskin

---

122

Have Fun Despite the Naysayers

When you work with complainers, it's hard to work up the nerve to celebrate anything positive in the office. But that's exactly what you should do: Focus on the positive. Celebrate promotions, birthdays for those who still acknowledge them, impending weddings or births. Don't let the occupants in the "ahem" corner discourage you from providing a temporary reprieve from their moodiness.

> ### Assignment
>
> Send out an e-mail asking colleagues to pick the best date for the next party.

Just observe a few etiquette rules to avoid giving the naysayers something else to complain about. Establish a suggested minimum for the collection envelope. Be reasonable so that people don't feel plundered. As an alternative you could ask people to bring in food.

On the day of the party start promptly so you don't have knots of people just milling around and keep the noise to a minimum so you don't disturb the colleagues who are determined to work rather than attend an office party.

After the party don't forget to send out an e-mail thanking all who contributed and helped brighten the office atmosphere, if only for a day.

Epilogue

Defy the office whiners. Celebrate!

123

Beware the "Mind Reader"

Every office has an employee who purports to know the boss better than anyone else. People wear such claims with an air of authority to keep other employees in check. A colleague I served on a project with was, hands down, the favorite of a manager. She once shot down an idea of mine with a claim that she knew the boss wouldn't buy it. She was adamant in her objections until I reminded her that I had known the supervisor much longer than she had. And I was eager to discuss my idea with him without the interference of a self-appointed interpreter.

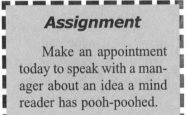

Assignment

Make an appointment today to speak with a manager about an idea a mind reader has pooh-poohed.

The special-access claim is nothing more than a power play. It makes the employee seem more powerful than she is. The person may even offer to take your concerns to the boss because she knows how to approach the manager.

The best thing you can do is to decline such an offer. You don't need anyone to do your bidding with the boss. You are your best advocate.

Epilogue

When it comes to dealing with the boss don't let second-hand stories from so-called intermediaries do your talking.

124

Prep for a Meeting With the Boss

When you finally decide to enlist a manager's help in dealing with an office foe, approach the meeting like a manager. Ask the supervisor ahead of time how much time he or she can spare. Prepare a script or outline, particularly if you're nervous, so that you cover your points and respect the manager's time constraints.

Assignment

List in a spiral notebook or a computer file the points you want to discuss with the boss about a difficult coworker. Rank them in importance.

Prioritize your comments and anticipate follow-up questions, advises Marie McIntyre in *Secrets to Winning at Office Politics: How to achieve your goals and increase your influence at work.* "Start with your most important points," she says, "and move quickly but be prepared for them to pepper you with questions after about three sentences. Executives don't want to listen to a monologue."

Be concise. You'll frustrate a manager if the person has to help you both focus and provide a solution. Tell the supervisor how you've tried to combat the problem. And advise him or her of other options you're considering, especially unpalatable ones. Stress that you are hoping he or she can suggest better ones.

Most importantly, show how the constant battling affects your work. Don't deal in personalities during such talks. You will come across as unprofessional.

> ### Epilogue
> *Solid groundwork will help you put your best foot forward in a meeting with a manager.*

Flu Rage

Employees who come to work sick are often misguided. "Tenacious" and "dedicated" are how they might describe their efforts. Increasingly though, their colleague and others would use quite different terms. Economists call this dogged persistence "presenteeism," and it costs companies bundles in productivity losses.

On-the-job productivity losses from presenteeism account for as much as 60 percent of employers' total

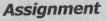

> ### *Assignment*
>
> If your company grants few sick days off, ask permission to start a pool allowing those with unused sick days to donate some to those who are ill and have no sick days left.

costs related to workers' illnesses, according to a joint study by Cornell University and the health-information firm Medstat.

Sometimes colleagues drag themselves in because they've exhausted their sick days or the company didn't offer the benefit in the first place. Still, politely suggest to sick colleagues that they stay home so they can rest up. Point out that not only do they risk infecting others, but they won't get much done.

If the colleagues persist in coming to work with raging fevers or ferocious coughs, speak with a manager. Even consider using the talk as an opportunity to lobby for more sick days. Maybe your company needs to offer more sick days to keep the office healthy.

Epilogue

"Healing is a matter of time, but it is sometimes also a matter of opportunity."—Hippocrates

---

126

Beware the Manipulator

Some coworkers love the manipulation game. Too often the strings they attach to friendship aren't visible until a big blow-up lays them bare. That's when you realize that beneath their attitude of extraordinary servitude and forbearance lies the heart of a puppeteer. One of their unspoken messages is: "If I am going to go out of my way for you, even avoid disagreeing with you, you should return the favor."

Assignment

Follow the famous Nordstrom rules for its employees: Rule Number 1: Use your own good judgment in all situations. Rule Number 2: There will be no additional rules.

A coworker became incensed when I disagreed with her about the origins of the English language. She insisted English was a Latin-derived language because it contained so many Latin words. It's a Germanic language, I stressed. She told me I was dead wrong and stormed off.

That rocky exchange made me realize the high price of her friendship. In exchange for it, I wasn't supposed to disagree with her. It was too high a price for me.

The best way to handle the manipulator is with even-handedness. Don't go along with them because they are the nicest people in the world, or seem to be. State your honest opinion. That will expose their strings every single time.

Epilogue

Friendships with steep price tags are no bargain.

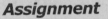

The Art of the Riposte

The clever comeback, like humor, works magic in battles with adversaries. With wit as your weapon you can defuse a tense situation. You lighten up. You trim your enemy's sails and maybe even make the person smile.

When the high-minded food police publicly assault your culinary choices, borrow a Peter Burns line: "You are what you eat, and who

Assignment

Keep your mind primed for clever comebacks by noting ripostes you've overheard or read. Refer to them from time to time to keep them fresh in your mind. Consider Dr. Mardy Grothe's book *Viva la Repartee: Clever comebacks & witty retorts from history's great wits & wordsmiths.*

wants to be a lettuce?" Or try "Hunger is not debatable," a line attributed to Harry Hopkins.

We all have the capacity for killer lines. The problem is that most of us think of clever comebacks after the fact. Those Johnny-come-lately responses are what the French call "staircase wit." They come to you as you descend the stairs at evening's end.

Granted some people seem to be a natural for such comebacks, but maybe they just worked harder to acquire the skill. And the art of the riposte is a skill.

If you want to acquire it then you have to make the effort consistently.

Epilogue

Add quips to your quiver. Your opponent won't know what hit him.

128

Red Alert: A Colleague Belittles You in Front of the Boss

Some opponents are fond of surgical strikes. The dictionary defines such attacks as usually without warning and intended for a specific target. They're potent, especially when the strike hits its mark—you—in front of the boss.

In the attacker's mind, the smaller you look in front of the boss the bigger she will appear. So while the boss is chatting informally with a group including you and your assailant, she will gleefully point out that you left a cover sheet off a report but she took care of the oversight. She will also mention that the phone numbers you passed along were outdated and slowed down her attempts to contact a former client. All of this is information that could have waited for a private conversation, but it can't for someone determined to put you in the worst light.

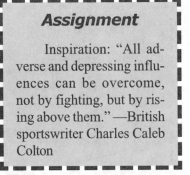
The best way to neutralize this extreme form of unprofessional behavior is the highest order of professionalism. Thank the accuser for helping you out. Tell her you expect you will have to return the favor some day, and you gladly will. As for the so-called erroneous information, say you will recheck the information for errors. But give your accuser a homework assignment. Ask her to make sure she wrote down the correct numbers. Then tell her that if you are in error, you will gladly send along information that corrects the problem. After that, resume your conversation with the boss. That seamless approach will put you in the best light.

Epilogue
Your enemies will never accuse you of acting too professionally.

129

Oh Perfection Most Foul

The only colleague I ever heard harp on statistics about minimum workout times was a devout couch potato. He planned

> ### Assignment
>
> For inspiration: "Striving for excellence motivates you; striving for perfection is demoralizing."
> —psychologist and management consultant Harriet Braiker

to meet that daily minimum some day—then 45 minutes—for the perfect workout. But because he couldn't go from 0 to 45 perfectly, the only workout he opted for was working his remote.

That's how perfectionism often works. It can be downright paralyzing. And when you're partnered with a perfectionist the result can be a working relationship that is far from perfect.

Their perfectionism usually means they have a difficult time meeting deadlines because their quest for perfection adds unnecessary time to their work. Their fear of making a wrong decision leaves them indecisive. Trying to reach a consensus could exhaust you.

For your own peace of mind, you'll have to take an active role in assuring the project's success. Suggest an outline and pacing to build momentum.

Tell the perfectionist that you appreciate the great care he takes with his work, but remind him that work that comes in late is far from perfect.

Epilogue
Perfectionism often has little to recommend it.

130

Play to Their Strengths

In his book *The Four Agreements: A practical guide to personal freedom*, Don Miguel Ruiz says that one of the four keys to a happy life is to be "impeccable with your word." In other words, always deliver on your promises. People who don't keep their word can be a source of utter frustration in the workplace.

Chris has a hard time enduring committee meetings because people don't keep their word. The head of a committee he was asked to serve on distributed a packet of material she wanted the group to review before the first meeting. On the day of the meeting, one colleague

came in extremely late and some of the others hadn't bothered to read the materials. Chris wanted to shout, "Why don't you stop wasting my time!"

You can't change your colleagues, but you can change how you relate to them so that you get more than disappointment out of your working relationships. Make suggestions that will play to colleagues' strengths rather than their weaknesses.

A colleague with strong research skills but poor writing skills might be the perfect partner on a two-person project as long as you both can agree you'll direct the writing. A capable colleague who tends to arrive late to meetings should be allotted time at the end of the meeting to present a report, rather than at the beginning. We all have our strengths and weaknesses. You'll experience a lot less frustration if you play to the promises your colleagues can keep.

Epilogue

Frustration plays to a colleague's weaknesses; effectiveness plays to the person's strength.

131

Ouch! The Supersensitive Colleague

Thin-skinned colleagues will keep you on the ropes if you allow them to. These employees typically have low self-esteem and see slights in everything you do. Everything unpleasant that happens to them is seen as a deliberate act done by you or someone else.

Assignment

Write this on a 3 × 5 card for inspiration: "When the price of forgiveness is too steep, learn to live without it."

I forgot to return a former colleague's phone call. She was having a difficult time landing a job and needed some information from me. She accused me of being arrogant for not calling her back. But the call had simply slipped my mind. When I did call, I couldn't convince her otherwise.

We all have moments like that. And most people we accidentally shortchange slough off the oversights. But oversights equal outright slights in the mind of the oversensitive colleague.

If you land on such a person's list of undesirables, apologize. Then ask if you can help now. If the person hurls a vengeful, "No!" then tell the person you are ready to move on. And do just that.

Epilogue

You can never win with supersensitive colleagues. Their goal lines keep changing.

132

When You're Asked to Clean Up a Colleague's Report

You may be asked to rescue inferior work performed by a coworker. If you don't handle the situation with finesse, that colleague could go from friend to foe in an instant.

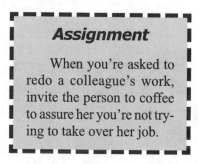

Assignment

When you're asked to redo a colleague's work, invite the person to coffee to assure her you're not trying to take over her job.

You can't count on the manager who requested the do-over to smooth any ruffled feathers. He or she often is looking for the easiest path to getting work done. So the supervisor may not ask your coworker for a revision. Instead, you'll inherit the assignment. When that happens, you'll have to walk a tight rope between meeting your boss's expectations and preserving your coworker's friendship.

Ask the manager if you can inform the colleague of your assignment. When you talk with your coworker, tell her you'll gladly give her a copy of your revision. If parts of the report were well done, pass that news along to both your colleague and your boss. And try to answer honestly your colleague's questions about why the project was handed to you. That honesty could well be the glue that keeps the friendship intact.

Epilogue

Even when you have marching orders, you have to work to avoid making enemies of friends along the way.

133

Listen Up

The health of a company's bottom line depends on how well its employees work as a unit to produce the quality of goods and services they wouldn't be able to produce individually. To make that process work, you and your coworkers must master the art of the compromise. Compromising with a bully or other office troublemakers is something you probably swore you'd never do. But in your gut you know you have to.

Assignment

On a piece of paper, dissect a long-simmering dispute with a colleague and try to tease out a compromise.

A key element of the art of compromising is understanding what your opponent is saying.

"Seek first to understand and then to be understood," author Stephen Covey says in *The Seven Habits of Highly Effective People.*

Listen to your foe's argument. Then put forth yours. Choose the best from the two and you'll have a new, richer starting point you both can claim ownership to.

Epilogue

Compromising is Latin for "to promise mutually." That mutuality is the secret of great teamwork.

Where's My Stapler?

The cubicled office reflects different things to different people. Consider office supplies. To chronic borrowers the wide openness of a cube farm represents a veritable self-serve bazaar of office supplies. It doesn't matter that the supplies reside on someone's desk.

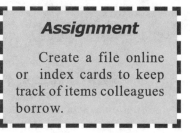

Assignment

Create a file online or index cards to keep track of items colleagues borrow.

Serial borrowers don't see boundaries. Plus, they swear to themselves that they will return the items promptly. Of course they never do. That's the root of the problem.

A colleague was so chronic with unauthorized borrowing that when people couldn't locate items, she was suspect No. 1. She was notorious for borrowing staplers and tape and not returning them. She had no idea how much she inconvenienced people who had to hunt down their own supplies.

If you spot your supplies on such a coworker's desk, retrieve them and drop him or her a firm but humorous note to press your point about respecting boundaries: "I don't mind authorized borrowing. But I do mind kidnapping."

Insist that the person ask your permission before removing things from your desk. Like a library, when colleagues borrow such things as books or magazines, limit the amount of time they can keep an item. Be sure to thank colleagues when they return items promptly. You want to encourage that behavior.

Epilogue

"Genius borrows nobly," said Ralph Waldo Emerson. And it lends nobly, too.

135

Admit When You're Wrong

Admitting to a mistake is probably the last thing you want to do in front of an office foe, but if you accuse someone of spreading a vicious rumor and the accusation later turns out to be false, you owe that person an apology. You may be tempted to resist the notion because you believe your colleague is incapable of the same consideration toward you. If you play by your nemesis's rulebook, you become like your nemesis.

You could pretend the incident never happened but that will only worsen your already strained relationship. What's more

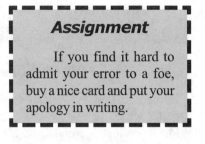

Assignment

If you find it hard to admit your error to a foe, buy a nice card and put your apology in writing.

your refusal to right your wrong will allow your nemesis to play the role of the aggrieved to the office. That's the last thing you want. "Put a rogue in the limelight and he will act like an honest man," Napoleon Bonaparte said.

Don't expect sympathy when you apologize. After all, the person is a thorn in your side that most likely won't transform into a rose bush just because you apologize. Don't let that bother you. The apology is mostly about you anyway. You demonstrate that you're honest and courageous enough to admit your faults.

Epilogue
Admitting a mistake to a foe is one of the most courageous things you can do.

You're Not Alone

Sometimes you find yourself coping with difficult colleagues no matter where you work, and you may wonder if the world has lost its collective mind. It hasn't. It's just rude and growing more so by the minute.

A study by the nonprofit group Public Agenda found that 79 percent of Americans believe that rudeness—defined as a lack of respect and courtesy—is so severe that it should be viewed as a national problem. And 60 percent believe the problem is worsening.

"Our society has contributed to people being more rude," said Karen A. Solomon, a psychotherapist in Commack, New York.

Working women certainly feel the pressures that lead to discourtesies. "They are rushing to work, picking up kids, taking kids to appointments, and rushing home. They just have so much to do that they lose sight of common courtesies," she said.

Studies have cited other reasons for the increase in incivilities: increased workloads and fears about layoffs. Companies' fondness for outsourcing jobs and getting more out of their remaining employees, suggests the rudeness problem will get worse.

So don't blame yourself for difficult colleagues. Just make sure you don what psychologists call your "emotional wet suit" before heading into the office.

> ### Assignment
>
> Follow this advice: "Nothing in life is to be feared. It is only to be understood." —Marie Claire

---

Epilogue

You can leave a job but you'll never run away from difficult coworkers.

Beware the Minimizers

Allison had second thoughts about how she judged a colleague, Jessica, who was dressed down by a cube-mate for talking too loudly. The woman told Jessica that she was loud and inconsiderate. When Jessica told Allison how mean she thought the woman was, Allison just chalked it all up to a misunderstanding because it was true that her friend tended to talk loudly. Allison encouraged her to patch things up with the woman.

> **Assignment**
>
> "Empathy before judgment." Ask your artistically inclined son or daughter to make you a bookmark that incorporates those words.

That seemed like a good idea until Allison herself hit the woman's buzz saw. She couldn't hear while speaking with a client on the phone because the infamous shusher was holding a loud conversation with someone. She asked them to tone it down. The shusher loudly proclaimed that Allison demanded considerations she wasn't willing to return.

It became clear to her that the woman was indeed "mean" as her friend had concluded. Allison felt bad for not being more supportive of Jessica and later apologized.

Few people will be truly empathetic when you are going through a crisis. If you are lucky you'll have a colleague like Allison who will give her response a second look.

Mostly likely, though, you'll run into judgmental people who will continuously minimize your pain.

You can't do anything about that, but you can avoid allowing their shortsightedness to get the best of you. If they don't agree with you, it's not the end of the world. Sooner or later they may come around when they see a tyrant in a different light.

Epilogue

Unless you're dealing with weight loss, beware the minimizers.

138

Focus on the Good

A former colleague loved to pass along story ideas. He was well read, knew a lot, and liked being up on everything. His insecurity, however, prevented him from accepting suggestions from others. He dismissed others' story ideas as dated, unimportant, or irrelevant. I bristled many times when he labeled my ideas as such. At one point, I came close to never accepting another suggestion from him.

But then I realized how foolish that strategy would be. Why would I cut myself off from a reliable source of solid ideas? I decided, instead, to the keep that supply line open. If he wanted to cut himself off from sources of stories, that was an issue for him—and possibly his shrink—to wrestle with, not me.

Assignment

Write down an irritating employee's good points and bad points. See if you can maintain a cordial relationship by focusing on the good.

Epilogue

When it comes to dealing with coworkers, the "all-or-nothing" strategy can work against you.

When a Foe Asks for a Favor

Because the need to exchange information is constant in an office, sooner or later a nemesis will ask for your help. Retrieving the information may be easy. Deciding whether to share it is another thing.

Here's a good rule of thumb: If the information the person requests will help him or her do her job, then share it. Professionally, you want to be seen as a facilitator not an obstructionist, as your colleague might be. If your manager knows of the strained relationship between you and the difficult employee, let him or her know in a gentle way that you rose above your difficult relationship to help.

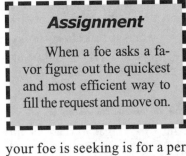

Assignment

When a foe asks a favor figure out the quickest and most efficient way to fill the request and move on.

If the information your foe is seeking is for a personal matter, you'll have to evaluate whether you want to be helpful. Then, you'll have no moral obligation to provide a helping hand to someone who's done nothing but slap it.

Epilogue

When a foe needs a favor to get a job done, remember that professionalism dictates that you lend a hand.

140

Handling the Over-indulger

If you've observed a colleague at an office party having a number of drinks or acting as if he's imbibed too much, alert a supervisor. Many companies make arrangements for employees who have overindulged. They will pay for a taxi ride home or spring for a hotel room. Offering just strong coffee and a wave good-bye doesn't cut it.

"Only time can make someone sober," according to Mothers Against Drunk Driving.

Though companies often require some supervisors to be on the lookout for intoxicated employees at festive functions, it helps if subordinates are on the alert as well.

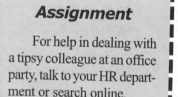

Assignment

For help in dealing with a tipsy colleague at an office party, talk to your HR department or search online.

Before going to a supervisor, try to discourage the colleague from further drinking by asking if you can get him some fruit juice or soda.

Don't let the difference in your ages or seniority prevent you from informing a supervisor about your inebriated colleague. And the day after, assure the person that you only wanted to help, and won't gossip about the incident. The person may be too ashamed to thank you then, but that doesn't mean they aren't grateful for your heroic efforts in quite possibly saving his life and his job.

Epilogue

Few people have ever regretted preventing a drunken colleague from taking to the road.

141

Asking a Fellow Manager to Respect Your Subordinates

An office manager wrote to me to describe a situation in her office that the doctor in charge refused to address. A new partner had repeatedly offered to give a young woman a ride home. She accepted once, but she was so put off by his aggressive behavior she wanted nothing to do with him after that. Still he persisted with the offers and often went over to her desk and stood uncomfortably close. She confided in the office manager. The officer manager, in turn, asked her boss, the doctor who owned the practice, to speak with the other doctor. The doctor in charge didn't. The young woman quit and now the office manager wonders if the ex-employee will sue.

When you're asked to address a fellow manager's inappropriate behavior, the problem won't go away if you do nothing. In fact, it could get worse if an employee sues.

When asked to speak with a fellow manager about his behavior toward your sub-

Assignment

Resolve to have a difficult conversation with a fellow manager. Write down the major points you want to cover.

ordinates, he may attempt to throw you off track by accusing you of indulging your workers. Just tell him you're not there to argue that point. Tell him to stop the behavior. That's your goal. Everything else is gibberish.

Epilogue
Confronting a fellow manager for abusive behavior is one of the toughest things you'll ever do. Not confronting the person could produce some of your biggest regrets.

142

The Disappearing Colleague

An accountant who worked in a small company disappeared for several hours each afternoon. He never announced why he needed to take off and never bothered to see if his coworkers might need financial information while he was out. When he returned, he conscientiously worked into the evening to make up the time. And that schedule suited his night owl lifestyle. But it frustrated the woman who wrote me for advice because he was often out when the office needed to confer with him.

When you have to depend on such inconsiderate coworkers, try to agree on a deadline for submitting information you both can live with. For emergencies ask him to check his cell phone in case the office needs to contact him.

If the person repeatedly disappears and fails to deliver vital information the boss requested, then pass along what you have with a note that says the other employee's contri-

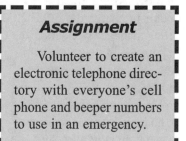

Assignment

Volunteer to create an electronic telephone directory with everyone's cell phone and beeper numbers to use in an emergency.

bution was unavailable. That could prompt action to cut down on the afternoon constitutionals.

Epilogue

Some employees have no compunction about leaving their colleagues in the lurch. Find ways to keep that insensitivity from affecting you.

143

When a Problem Employee Becomes Your Boss

If ever there were a workplace equivalent of Purgatory, you enter it when your worst nightmare becomes your supervisor.

It could happen. Many companies promote people despite their shortcomings, including an obvious lack of people skills.

Just half the business executives surveyed by DDI, a global human-resources consulting firm, said they were satisfied with their company's efforts to develop leaders. And only 61 percent considered themselves skilled enough to "bring out the best in people."

You best offense will be your best defense in handling the coworker-from-hell cum boss-from-hell. Meet with the manager and ask what you can do to make his job easier. Your new situation will call for managing up to avoid problems you may have had with the new supervisor in the past. When you have an idea, publicly attach your name to it as soon as possible. Write

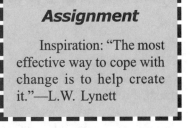

Assignment

Inspiration: "The most effective way to cope with change is to help create it."—L.W. Lynett

a memo to your boss explaining the idea and if necessary send a copy to other supervisors, with the idea of sharing. Being proactive might be your best weapon for dealing with the same old foe that has changed his title but maybe not his stripes.

Epilogue

When a foe becomes your boss, manage up to make the relationship work.

144

Demand Reciprocity

Some coworkers live according to a reverse beatitude: "It is better to receive than to give." They expect others to accommodate them but doing the reverse seldom occurs to them.

Rafael worked for a communications company that received business books for review. A colleague who collected books for his local library often stopped by Rafael's department to check the remainder table for extras. Rafael even held back some copies for the guy. He gleefully accepted them.

One day when Rafael was up against a deadline, he desperately needed the telephone number of a well-known researcher. He learned that the book collector would most likely have it. Rafael called him. The book collector said he too busy to look up the number. It wasn't as if he said, "I'll get back to you." He completely brushed Rafael off. From that point on Rafael didn't go out of his way to set aside books. He had assumed that reciprocity defined the relationship. But it was one way all along.

In order to build healthy relationships at work, you must insist on reciprocity. Otherwise, you will feel used.

> *Assignment*
>
> When someone returns a favor, send a card or e-mail to note how much you appreciate their thoughtfulness.

Epilogue

To build an honest relationship with a coworker, insist on reciprocity.

145

The Rosebush Cometh

A public-relations man who often breezed through a newspaper office to pitch stories about his clients was more noteworthy for his cologne than his ideas. The liberally applied cologne announced his arrival and unfortunately didn't depart until long after he had. The cologne generated a lot of discussion after he left, but no one worked up the nerve to ask him to tone down the dreadful scent.

Overly citrused, lilaced, or rosed people are weapons of mass distraction in the workplace. They, however, are often the last to know the maddening effects of their cologne or perfumes. Scents today are stronger because their creators want them to linger. So a little bit goes a long way. Too many people fail to realize that.

Assignment

If you can't work up the nerve to ask a colleague to tone down his cologne, send an anonymous letter with a polite request.

It's acceptable to speak up. What you shouldn't do is issue an order. As in, "I'm allergic and please don't wear that cologne again." Instead, try humor to get your request across. "Do they sell that stuff by the quart?" Or if you're allergic to the scents simply ask the wearer if he would consider wearing less. And thank him for hearing you out.

Epilogue

"Under the freedoms guaranteed by the First Amendment, is smelling up the place a constitutionally protected form of expression?" —Writer Calvin Trillin

146

Just Say No to the Office Peddler

I know people who have been pounced on in the office to buy cookies, candies, vitamins, kitchen utensils, make-up, and even beef, the latter from a former co-worker who retired to a farm.

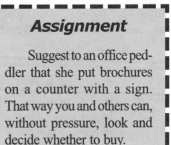

Assignment

Suggest to an office peddler that she put brochures on a counter with a sign. That way you and others can, without pressure, look and decide whether to buy.

In an office setting the pressure to buy from the office peddler can be great. If others are buying you may fear being labeled the office miser if you don't bite. The same guidelines for responsible shopping should apply to buying in the office. If you don't need or want what a coworker is selling, then don't buy.

If you buy under pressure you will feel resentful if that colleague later declines to buy Girl Scout cookies from your daughter.

To take the pressure off, ask the hawker to let you read over any materials the person has. And tell him or her you'll let them know if you're interested.

Epilogue

Whether out of the office or in, you and you alone should decide how your money is spent.

147

You're the Boss Now

About the sweetest ending to your long-running battle with a nemesis is a promotion that makes you his supervisor.

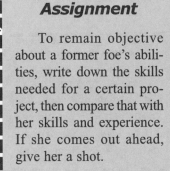

You'd be tempted to wield power to get back at the person for all the pain and misery she caused you. How tempting it would be to give her the worse assignments or evaluations or to ignore her requests for help with her own nemesis.

Don't manage based on the past or what you presume will happen in the future. You're calling the shots in the relationship. Act like it. As with anybody else you supervise, give out assignments based on skills, not anger. But make it clear than until the employee does something to improve the people skills she so sorely lacks certain assignments will always be off limits.

Assignment

To remain objective about a former foe's abilities, write down the skills needed for a certain project, then compare that with her skills and experience. If she comes out ahead, give her a shot.

Epilogue

When you become the boss of a nemesis, start the new relationship on a positive note going forward.

148

If the Boss Asks, Give an Honest Assessment of a Colleague

If you're asked to give your opinion about a difficult coworker, always give an honest assessment. It helps a manager to decide what needs to be fixed and what needs to be left alone.

That information is probably more valuable than you think. If the executive is asking, chances are the person plans to act on the information. Many executives do.

Be honest. Stick to the facts. An unjustifiably nega-

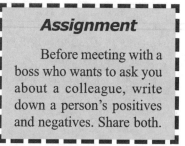

Assignment

Before meeting with a boss who wants to ask you about a colleague, write down a person's positives and negatives. Share both.

tive or positive assessment will serve no one, least of all you. If you exaggerate your remarks, a manager will realize he can't depend on you for the unvarnished truth.

If the colleague overall doesn't work well on a team or is unreliable, the inquiring supervisors should hear that. Similarly, if the person excels at something, bring that to the manager's attention, too. Make your opinion count when it matters most.

Epilogue
"To be honest is nothing; the reputation of it is all."
—William Congreve

149

If You Must, Avoid Contentious Topics

After a lively departmental meeting broke up, Kenneth and some colleagues continued the discussion in small groups in the hallway. A coworker walked up to Kenneth's group and barged into the conversation. He rattled off his strong views, then turned and hurried away. The group was speechless. They at least expected he would stay to hear their take on the topic. Clearly, he wasn't interested in any other views.

Some colleagues border on fanatics when it comes to certain topics. And they have

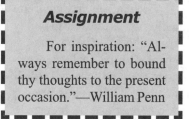

Assignment

For inspiration: "Always remember to bound thy thoughts to the present occasion."—William Penn

no tolerance for disagreement. They will either become agitated, attack the dissenter, or simply storm off. Their uncompromising take on life can run the gamut of topics that include child rearing, dieting, exercise, religion, or politics.

Some people think it takes great courage to wade into a contentious discussion to try to convert a stalwart. And shying away from controversial topics strikes them as cowardice. The opposite is true. It takes great courage to accept that you can't have a rational discussion with a colleague who has a clamp on his mind. So once you find the person's touchy-topic buttons, avoid them like the plague.

Epilogue
Steer clear of certain topics with fanatical coworkers.

150

Assemble an Emotional First-Aid Kit

When you work with difficult people, going to work can seem like the equivalent of going to war. So make sure you always pack an emotional first-aid kit. That kit would offer a ready array of strategies for picking your way through an office battlefield.

Though you may have considered a number of items separately, now is the time to pull them all together like a grand buffet. During really tense times, imagine yourself loading the kit into your brief case or bag as you prepare to leave for work.

Your kit's basics should include information on the

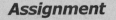

Assignment

On a 3 × 5 card write the tools you can stock your emotional tool kit with.

following: Office safe havens where you can go to reflect after an intense encounter, allies to turn to for advice and support, and strategies to help you remain calm in the heat of battle. You should make an effort to consciously tap into that kit during the day as a reminder of all the resources at your fingertips. With an emotional toolbox you'll have more success picking the right tool for battle.

Epilogue

"Greatness lies not in being strong, but in the right using of strength."—Author and minister Henry Ward Beecher

151

When the Best Strategy Is to Move On

Sometimes your company's culture clashes with your values, particularly a culture that tolerates such things as incompetence or bullying. When the culture won't adapt to accommodate your values it's time to move on. Try to take the decision to leave out of the emotional realm. If you become tangled in your emotions, you will feel selfish for leaving a good job. Sit down and list the reasons for going and for staying. Base your decision on the cold hard numbers.

> ### *Assignment*
>
> Update your resume, start searching help-wanted ads online and in newspapers. Attend some networking sessions of trade groups to get a line on a new job.

You're not the first person to leave a job because of difficult coworkers, and you will not be the last. Difficult colleagues and managers are two big reasons that people flee companies. If the company's culture breeds boorish behavior toward women or minorities, it's time to move on. If despite your protests to management, a foe resumes inappropriate behavior toward you it's time to leave and seek redress from the outside.

Having to fight the same battle repeatedly is a sign that you're working in an environment that clashes with your values. As your last act, you should draw up an exit strategy.

Epilogue

When you feel out of place for all the wrong reasons, it's time to move on.

Index

About the Author

Carrie Mason-Draffen is a reporter and columnist for Newsday, a daily newspaper based on Long Island, New York. She writes the newspaper's syndicated "Help Wanted" column, which runs in several papers throughout the country. Through her column she has helped hundreds of employees and managers to find solutions to difficult workplace problems. She lives on Long Island with her husband and their three teenagers.